Edited by Judy Verseghy and Sam Abel

Heavy Burdens

Stories of Motherhood and Fatness

DEMETER

Heavy Burdens
Stories of Motherhood and Fatness
Edited by Judy Verseghy and Sam Abel

Demeter Press
140 Holland Street West
P. O. Box 13022
Bradford, ON L3Z 2Y5
Tel: (905) 775-9089
Email: info@demeterpress.org
Website: www.demeterpress.org

Demeter Press logo based on the sculpture "Demeter" by Maria-Luise Bodirsky
www.keramik-atelier.bodirsky.de

Printed and Bound in Canada

Front cover artwork Sid Robitaille (Sitka). Front cover font Trevor Kai.
Typesetting Michelle Pirovich

Library and Archives Canada Cataloguing in Publication
Heavy burdens : stories of motherhood and fatness / Judy Verseghy and Sam
Abel, editors.
Includes bibliographical references.
ISBN 978-1-77258-174-4 (softcover)
1. Motherhood--Social aspects. 2. Overweight women. 3. Obesity in women.
4. Overweight children. 5. Obesity in children. 6. Discrimination against
overweight persons. 7. Obesity--Psychological aspects. 8. Obesity--
Social aspects.
I. Verseghy, Judy, 1982-, editor II. Abel, Sam, 1990-, editor

MIX
Paper from
responsible sources
FSC
www.fsc.org   FSC® C004071

Acknowledgments

We would like to thank Demeter Press and Andrea O'Reilly for supporting this manuscript and offering invaluable guidance, May Friedman for her review and mentorship throughout this process, and all of the maternal and fat activists who came before us for paving the way. Finally we would like to thank the contributors for sharing their stories, art, and research with us. It has been a privilege to work with all of you.

Judy would like to thank Sam for joining her on this wild ride, and for her patience, organizational skill, and attention to detail—without Sam, this vision would never have come to fruition. Thanks to Jane for her boundless creativity in capturing an essence in just a few short words. Huge thanks to Nathan for his endless support, in this and all of my endeavours. Thank you to my parents for giving me the education I needed to arrive to the point where this book could be made. Finally, thank you to my mother for always doing her thoughtful best, and to Seth, Iz, and Zoe for encouraging me to do mine.

Sam would like to thank Trevor, Crystal, Amie, and Judy for supporting her through the process of bringing this anthology from conception to completion. Thank you all for your encouragement and feedback as I worked through how to explore my relationship with my mother, and the challenges of putting those explorations into print.

This work is dedicated to the members of The Village, who make us feel safe, challenge our minds, and fill our bellies.

Contents

Introduction
Judy Verseghy and Sam Abel
11

Section I
Baby Weight: Pregnancy and Fatness
17

Chapter One
The Elephant in the Room:
Naming Fatphobia in Maternity Care
George Parker and Cat Pausé
19

Bearing
Emma Day
33

Chapter Two
Overfeeding the Floating Fetus and Future Citizen:
The "War on Obesity" and the Expansion of Fetal Rights
April Herndon
35

Chapter Three
Eating for Two: The Fear and Threat of Fatness in Pregnancy
Megan Davidson and Sarah Lewin
45

Beauty in the Eye of Eternity
Sid Robitaille (Sitka)
61

Chapter Four
Goal Weights, Planned Parenthood, and Aging Past My Prime:
A Reproductive Timeline
Emily R.M. Lind
63

Section II: (Don't) Let Them Eat Cake
Experiences of Fat Kids
77

Chapter Five
I am not Small
deborah schnitzer
79

Love Always
bathbunny
95

Chapter Six
Conversations with Our Mothers: Exploring Maternal Blame
and the Generational Effects of Body Management
Samantha Walsh and Jen Rinaldi
97

Untitled
R.A.
109

Chapter Seven
Esau: Curse, Stare, Courage
Natasha Galarraga
111

Chapter Eight

Dear Mom

Sam Abel

117

Chapter Nine

Happiness Projects and Close Bonds:

A Calorie-Counting Mother and Her Fat, Feminist Killjoy Daughter

Crystal Kotow

137

Section III: Coming to Term(s):

Fat Motherhood

147

Sky Woman, Mother

Emma Day

149

Chapter Ten

From Famine to Feast:

Pregnancy and Motherhood

Liz Nelson

151

Sharing

Emma Day

153

Chapter Eleven

Crazy, Squishy Love: How I Learned to Love

My Body through the Eyes of my Son

Jodi Christie

155

Feeding
Emma Day
159

Chapter Twelve
Mother to Daughter:
From Fat Hatred to Fat Love in One Hundred Years
Jennifer Lee
161

Chapter Thirteen
Exoskeleton
Sherezada Windham-Kent
171

Smiling
Emma Day
181

Chapter Fourteen
The Fat of the Matter:
Fat Activist Parenting in Fatphobic Times
Judy Verseghy
183

Chapter Fifteen
Passing It On
Kimberly Dark
187

Notes on Contributors
195

Introduction

Judy Verseghy and Sam Abel

In the current sociopolitical climate, both mothering and "obesity"[1] are sites of panic, blame, and regulation. The increased pressure on individual mothers and fat people obscures larger structural issues of racism, sexism, ableism, economic inequality, and fatphobia. In this anthology, we hope to shed light on these issues, and how fatness shapes the experiences of both mothers and children, for better or worse.

This anthology draws on academic and personal material focusing on "women" and "mothers." The authors and editors, however, acknowledge that pregnant people and parents do not always identify with these highly gendered terms. Sex and gender are complex; they do not exist in binaries, and they cannot be determined via a quick analysis of reproductive organs. Similarly, mothering (the action) and motherhood (the institution) are not exclusive to individuals who identify as women, nor are they attributable to individuals who gave birth. All mothers—birth, adoptive, chosen, desired, familial, foster, estranged, or non-conforming—experience pressure, doubt, guilt, and responsibility associated with mothering in a neoliberal, patriarchal context.

As fat activists, we believe that fat embodiment is valid and to be celebrated. We chose the title *Heavy Burdens* to highlight the burdens and barriers socially imposed on fat people. In this book, fat mothers and children discuss the "heaviness" of the experiences of being fat—the ways in which we are read, received, and not accommodated. *Heavy Burdens* explores the implications of moving through the world as a fat mother or child, and its authors offer insightful and empathetic readings of their lived experiences and/or research.

When we first conceived of this book, we were not sure whether anyone would want to submit materials, yet the response was overwhelming, signalling that issues of motherhood and fatphobia resonate strongly in our communities. This anthology paints a rich picture of the nuanced ways in which motherhood and fatness intersect. Our authors approach this topic in a number of ways; they thoughtfully analyze the complexity of fatness and motherhood through academic work, creative submissions, and personal stories. The pieces expose the ever-present ideologies shaping the ways in which fat mothers and fat children are treated and the ways in which we treat ourselves, and each other. You will read stories of sadness, learning, triumph, or simply coming to term(s)—with varied embodiments, with relationships, and with challenging experiences. Perhaps you will even see yourself in some of the experiences documented here.

We have organized this book to shadow a journey through life. The imposition of fatphobic ideologies begins before birth, or even before conception, as you can see in the book's first section, "Baby Weight: Pregnancy and Fatness." George Parker and Cat Pausé's "'The Elephant in the Room': Naming Fatphobia in Maternity Care" gives voice to fat pregnant women in New Zealand, and exposes the ways in which they experience fatphobia as microagressions, medicalization, and overt shaming and bullying while seeking out prenatal care. April Herndon's "Overfeeding the Floating Fetus and Future Citizen: The 'War on Obesity' and the Expansion of Fetal Rights" examines the ways in which the dialogue surrounding fetal rights has been taken up in the context of fat management, where "fetal overnutrition" has become as vilified as illicit drug use during pregnancy. Megan Davidson and Sarah Lewin have seen the ways that these harmful and fear-inducing messages of fatphobia have impacted their clients in their New York City-based doula practice; in "Eating for Two: The Fear and Threat of Fatness in Pregnancy," they offer their insights and advocate for a weight-neutral approach in prenatal care. Finally, future pregnancies, fat futurities, and "fat time" shape Emily R.M. Lind's "Goal Weights, Planned Parenthood, and Aging Past my Prime: A Reproductive Timeline"—an autobiographical piece outlining the ways in which queer and fat embodiment shaped her experience of conception and pregnancy.

"(Don't) Let Them Eat Cake: The Experiences of Fat Kids," the second section, explores how fatphobia and fat embodiment impact parent-child relationships. Parents—most often, mothers—experience significant pressure via the medical industry and society at large to ensure that their children (and themselves) maintain a so-called healthy weight. Mothers who cannot keep themselves and their children thin are told that they have failed as individuals and as caregivers, which puts great pressure on mothers to judiciously perform a specific brand of body management. The authors in this section acknowledge this, and their contributions illustrate a standpoint of care and compassion for mothers, so many of whom have internalized messages that their own bodies are not good enough, while they try their best to support their children to live long and happy lives.

This section begins with deborah schnitzer's "I am not Small," which intertwines her poetry with lines from well-loved children's rhymes as she traces her relationship with her mother, herself, and both of their embodiments. Samantha Walsh and Jen Rinaldi engage with disability theory and maternal theory in "Conversations with our Mothers: Exploring Maternal Blame and the Generational Effects of Body Management"; they describe the ways in which their mothers' ideas and impositions around weight and consumption interacted with their experiences of disability. Using reflexive storytelling, Natasha Galarraga's "Esau: Curse, Stare, Courage" offers insight into her experiences with both fatness and polycystic ovary syndrome (PCOS), and the ways in which both categories affected her embodiment, her feelings of femininity, and her relationships with family members and friends. Sam Abel's graphic short story "Dear Mom" deftly illustrates the ways food and weight can be used as a proxy in relationships between mothers and daughters—being offered, withheld, or scrutinized—as a means to avoid engaging in more meaningful conversations. Finally, Crystal Kotow's "Happiness Projects and Close Bonds: A Calorie-Counting Mother and her Fat, Feminist Killjoy Daughter" considers weight loss as a "happy object," and explores the work involved in maintaining relationships between a fat-activist daughter and her consistently dieting mother.

In the anthology's third and final section, "Coming to Term(s): Fat Motherhood," our contributors trace the impact motherhood has had on their bodies and their relationships with their children and parents. This section opens with Liz Nelson's short but moving piece "From Famine to Feast: Pregnancy and Motherhood" which charts her experiences of unintentionally losing weight during pregnancy and regaining—and more—after her child was born. In "Crazy, Squishy

Love: How I Learned to Love My Body through the Eyes of My Son," Jodi Christie discusses her experiences with disordered eating, particularly how her relationship with food and her body changed over the course of her pregnancy and into motherhood, and how she navigates this relationship in the context of parenting. Jenny Lee's "Mother to Daughter: From Fat Hatred to Fat Love in One Hundred Years" traces how four generations of women in her family approach food and weight. In "Exoskeleton," Sherezada Windham-Kent uses humour to discuss the challenging ways in which motherhood and disability affected her clothing choices, and how that, in turn, affected her relationship with her fatness. In "The Fat of the Matter: Fat Activist Parenting in a Fatphobic World," Judy Verseghy continues the discussion around the intersections between body politics and parenting by examining the ways her childhood experiences and her discovery of fat activism intermingle and affect how she approaches issues of food and weight with her children. And finally, the anthology ends with Kimberly Dark's "Passing It On," where she offers insight into how children's relationships to food can be positively altered when they live in a diet-free home.

Beyond the chapters outlined above, you will also find a series of images created for this anthology by four powerful artists: Emma Day, R.A., Sid Robitaille (Sitka), and @bathbunny. Each image speaks strongly for itself, and we welcome you to take a moment to really consider the images included here, and what they mean for fat mothers and fat children.

We hope that each of these pieces offer new insights for you. We hope that they make you angry, sad, hopeful, compassionate, or relieved that it's not just you who has had these experiences and feelings. We hope that when you finish this book you feel better armed against the crushing ideologies of motherhood and pervasive fatphobia permeating our lives in the most subtle and insidious of ways. We hope your eyes are opened, or opened still, and that you can take what you have read and use it to your advantage. Finally, we hope you pass this book on to someone who may need it.

In solidarity,

Judy and Sam

Endnote

1 You will notice that the term "obesity" has been put into what are commonly referred to as scare quotes in some chapters in this book. These quotation marks serve to indicate that we reject the medicalization of fatness as "obesity." We challenge and critique the health-based and socially-driven negative associations that come with viewing fatness as a pathological state rather than a form of embodiment like any other.

Section I:
Baby Weight: Pregnancy and Fatness

Chapter One

The Elephant in the Room: Naming Fatphobia in Maternity Care

George Parker and Cat Pausé

"In any society, the way a woman gives birth and the kind of care given to her and the baby points as sharply as an arrowhead to the key values of the culture" (Kitzinger 115).

The dynamics and consequences of fatphobia in healthcare have been well established in research in recent years (Pausé; Phelan et al.; Puhl and Heuer). However, very little research has addressed women's[1] experiences of fatphobia in relation to reproductive and maternal healthcare. This is an oversight, since maternity care represents one of the longest exposures to healthcare services for women and their families, and is a profound and formative moment in their lives (Simkin). For fat pregnant people in Aotearoa, New Zealand, experiences with maternity care have included severely restricted birthing options, such as caregiver and place of birth, and the reorientation of population-wide "obesity-prevention" strategies to the new priority area of pregnant women, new mothers, and young children (Parker). In the cacophony of voices making claims about maternal fatness as a health issue, (e.g. Gluckman and Hanson; Heslehurst; Denison and Chiswick), the voices of fat pregnant women and new mothers themselves have been excluded. The silence of fat women in social and health discourse about their bodies allows the partial truths of medical science to stabilize into fact and makes invisible the ways in which fatphobia—intersecting with other oppressive social forces including sexism, racism, colonialism, and economic in-equalities—influences the health of pregnant women, new mothers, and their babies.

The narratives presented here are drawn from research undertaken in Auckland,[2] New Zealand, with twenty-seven ethnically diverse, cisgendered, and self-identified fat pregnant women and new mothers. They participated in one-on-one in-depth semistructured interviews with the first author (Parker). The objective of the research was to give voice to fat pregnant women and new mothers' experiences of fatphobia in maternity care. The interviews were undertaken as a caring conversation between the first author (who herself was visibly pregnant at the time) and participant, usually in the participant's home. This approach to narrative research acknowledges that narratives are created relationally; it aims to foster a caring relationship between the researcher and narrator (Frid et al.). We have organized these narratives into three groupings describing the various means by which fatphobia expresses itself in maternity care: fatphobia as microaggressions, fatphobia as medicalization, and fatphobia as overt shaming and bullying.

Fatphobia as Microaggressions

Our participants' narratives reveal the ways in which microaggressions toward fatness thread through the minutiae of everyday maternity care. Microaggressions, a term first used in critical race studies, describe "the everyday verbal, non-verbal, and environmental slights, snubs or insults, whether intentional or unintentional that communicate hostile, derogatory or negative messages to target persons based solely upon their marginalized group membership" (Sue 3). Microaggressions are usually delivered unconsciously by the well-intentioned, manifesting as small or even invisible slights that accumulate to have a powerful impact on the physical and psychological wellbeing of those oppressed by them (3). Expressions of "medical concern" by maternity caregivers—such as midwives, nurses, doctors, and others—along with physical maternity care environments that do not accommodate fat bodies functioned powerfully as fatphobic microaggressions in our study.

The women in our study embarked on pregnancy fully cognizant that they were fat, and they were alert to negative attitudes or judgments from maternity caregivers and others about their weight. This alertness was embedded in embodied histories constituted from a lifetime of fatphobic encounters both outside of and within health services that they had carried with them on their reproductive journeys. Skye[3] shared the following:

> I've been big my whole life, and you know you have it drilled into you so that being fat is so bad, you know? Like, I got bullied at school. My dad used to do awful things like make my favourite meal with me and then tell me I couldn't eat it. My whole life I've had all this, you know, some people are horrible. I could be in a car, and someone could just yell at me out the window, "you fat ..."or whatever. It does happen, and it's not a rare thing. So you, you carry this feeling of "fat is so horrible, and so disgusting" and then somebody like that, like a health professional, adds to that feeling, you carry it everywhere.

Though highly cognizant of their weight, participants described their surprise and distress at the extent to which their fatness was framed as a medical issue that posed risks to their pregnancy and future child in their first meetings with maternity caregivers. Participants described having their bodies weighed, measured, and visually assessed by their maternity carers resulting in open expressions of disdain and disapproval. Maternity caregivers' negative attitudes towards participants' fatness was framed both in terms of the potential complications that may arise during pregnancy and childbirth, as well as the burden of extra care and resources needed to manage those complications. Emma recounted her first encounter with a doctor after she discovered she was pregnant:

> We went to the doctor, and we were really happy, you know because of having a baby, and just the way he was towards us. We actually left in tears because he was acting as though it was a disaster; it was just really horrible. He just kept going on and on about my weight and all he would say was my size over and over. And he actually said that he thought that I should have an abortion and that was really upsetting to me because I would never have wanted to do that.

The power of "medical concern" as a microaggressive form of fatphobia is evidenced by how difficult it was for participants to question the problematization of their bodies even when this contradicted their own, often much more positive, view of themselves. Rather participants internalized the negative messages presented and took up responsibility for themselves as a risk to their babies and a burden on maternity services and caregivers. As Mel explored, this led some participants to question whether they even had a right to their pregnancies:

> It makes you feel like you're walking around with a little red dot on your head. Like in the community ... you've got this little arrow on you going "not only are you big in everyday life, but we have to look after you special because you've chosen to get yourself pregnant, and we're going to have to put extra resources towards you." So yeah, it makes you feel guilt, that you're taking away stuff from the health system that could be used elsewhere, instead because I have chosen to be a larger lady having a baby it's going to require more resources put into me, and they wouldn't have to do that if I was smaller.

The expression of fatphobia as medical concern is particularly pernicious in the context of maternity care because it pits the mother's body against her child's—undermining the development of a positive maternal identity. Our participants were left asking what kind of mother they would be if they had already risked harm to their developing baby. Rochelle shared the following:

> I was very, very worried. I was like oh my gosh; this is a bad thing that I've gone and got myself pregnant.... I wasn't thinking that I wasn't healthy enough.... But now that she's [midwife] telling me [that I'm too fat] I was like "oh no, what am I going to do, is this child going to come out deformed?" I was like "is my baby ... am I going to give it the right chance?"

Microaggressive expressions of fatphobia are also manifested in the physical environment of maternity services that do not accommodate fat bodies, which quietly signals that fat bodies do not belong there. These environmental slights include seating in waiting rooms and clinics that fat women cannot use; ill-fitting gowns, scales, blood-pressure cuffs, wheelchairs, and other hospital equipment; and posters and pamphlets in maternity services representing only slender mothers. Tali recounted her shame and embarrassment at not fitting into the hospital gown that she was given during labour:

> It was when I had to take off my clothes, like, they couldn't find a thing to fit me. I mean I didn't care, but it was just if, you would think that if they would see a larger person that you wouldn't bring a small gown, and you would go find the biggest, if that's the biggest, then that's the biggest, like instead of trying the small one, you might go, oh wait, I'll go get a bigger one ... it just made me feel, I'd rather stand there naked, you know?

Participants were alert to these quiet slights in the physical space of maternity care, yet their normalized and subtle nature made them difficult to challenge. Instead these slights added to the feeling of being a burden to maternity caregivers and to doubt that they should ever have become pregnant in the first place. As Maia described "Just the scales that weren't big enough for me, all the equipment, you know? You kinda get the sense when you're in the hospital that you're taking up a lot of space, that you're taking up more space than what's allocated to you." A number of participants mused at how easily the micro-aggressions wrought in the physical environments of maternity care could have been remedied with some forethought and care. Leilani described such an insight during her doctors' repeated attempts to use a small blood-pressure cuff on her arm:

> It's all the tools that they have and you know they do have bigger ones around but they always had to try to take my blood pressure with the small cuff and then have to take it off because it wouldn't do up, and then go get another one. And I wonder why they couldn't be prepared. If you know your next patient is someone bigger, maybe put all the little things that you don't need away and have the other ones ready for them so that you don't have to look around. And the patient doesn't feel like they're becoming a nuisance because you have to find all this gear for them because it doesn't fit.

Fatphobia as Medicalization

Fatphobia also manifests in the medicalization of fat women's pregnancies, which is based on the belief that fat is inherently pathological
and fat women are not capable of successfully growing and birthing
their babies without medical surveillance and management. Medicalization was a process rooted in maternity caregivers' inability to get past
the number on the scales and see the whole person. Participants
perceived that maternity caregivers made assumptions about everything
from their health, lifestyles, social contexts, and even their education
levels and intelligence based on their weight. Emma, who emphasized
her highly successful career, described the attitudes of maternity
caregivers at a prenatal hospital clinic she attended: "They just assumed
that I must be stupid, that I must be lazy, I must eat junk food, I mustn't
know anything about health, yeah, that just came through the whole
time." Ironically, the negative framing of their weight encountered in
maternity care was generally at odds with participants' much more
positive view of their general health and wellbeing. Participants'
described their struggle to reconcile the pathologization and
medicalization of their bodies with their own embodied sense of
wellness; they expressed frustration that their own views were neither
elicited nor believed by maternity caregivers. Lisa described the
following:

> And I went to one midwife, cause you know you can go to a few
> before you chose the right one, and she was like, "well you're not
> allowed to put on any weight." It was kind of the first thing she
> told me, and if I wanted to snack, I could snack on nuts. And I
> kind of went, "what?" So her whole focus was my weight; it
> wasn't about, you know she didn't really ask me what my diet
> was like, or what my exercise was like.

This failure to engage participants own knowledge led to the loss of
vital health promotion opportunities because many participants were
actively engaged in, or wanting to be engaged in, health-seeking
behaviours that could have been affirmed and supported if discussed.
Rather, the distribution of unsolicited weight- and diet-focused advice
to participants based on their visible fatness alone led to a sense of
frustration and annoyance with maternity caregivers. As Stacey admitted:
"when she [midwife] gave me those fliers for the exercise classes, I didn't

even want to look at them, because I was so upset and sort of offended by the way that she had approached the issue, that it almost made me want to rebel against her, and the information that she'd given me."

Reduced to a number on the scale that placed them in a medical risk category, participants described a cascade of medically imposed restrictions, surveillance, and interventions, which seemed to acquire momentum as they progressed through their pregnancies. Initial restrictions included limited or no choice at all about who would provide their care or where they could birth. Participants found themselves referred to high-risk prenatal clinics, and they were actively discouraged or explicitly barred from giving birth in low-risk birth environments—such as at home or birthing units, and smaller clinics appropriate for unmedicated births. This was particularly distressing for Māori[4] and Pasifika[5] participants who placed high priority on the ability to give birth in their local communities rather than being transferred to central city hospitals. Kahu, pregnant with her second baby, described her anger at being told she could not return to the local birthing centre where she had birthed her first child because she had gained weight between pregnancies: "They just assume that because you're fat you're going to have more problems, is that it? That's stupid; they just end up making the problems." Participants were also exposed to increased medical surveillance during their pregnancies including more than the usual number of blood tests, ultrasound scans, along with referrals for obstetric and anesthetic case reviews. In the course of these reviews, participants were informed of the risks their weight posed during childbirth, such as increased risk of Caesarean section and postpartum hemorrhage. They were encouraged to consent to the development of medical management plans for birth such as intravenous (IV line) access and early placement of epidural anesthesia. Participants described feeling fearful and disempowered as a result, setting aside their own aspirations for how they would give birth and submitting to medical management. As Ange described: "I remember my midwife was asking me about my birth plan and I said 'well, you know, the hospital's got my birth plan; it doesn't matter what I want.' And that's tough."

Participants felt that it was more often medical anxiety based on the generalized assumption that fat women could not healthily grow and birth their babies—rather than an accurate assessment of their individual circumstances—that fuelled the processes of medicalization to which they were exposed. This assumption of pathology led to a cascade of interventions resulting in highly medicalized births that many participants felt could have been avoided if they had been listened to and given individualized care. Participants described deep satisfaction when they birthed their babies without the medical intervention they were told they would likely need. Lisa described the experience of giving birth to her son at a central hospital having been refused access to her local birthing centre because of her weight:

> The hospital midwife was going "right, we need to get this drip in," because they were expecting me to have intravenous access to make a Caesarean easier, and I went to the toilet and I said, "oh," she was trying to stick it in and I was going "he's here!" And she was going "we'll just wait 'til we get this in," and I'm like "ah he's here." And she put her hand in the toilet and went "oh you just need to stand up love" [laughing], and I stood up and he just came out, waters and all. It was that fast. But it was the fact that they weren't listening to me, and they were so focused on getting the drip in my hand because of all these supposed complications and stress that I was going to have, and it's like, "ah he's here." Yeah, so for all their talk about how it was going to be this big Caesarean, and I wasn't going to be able to handle it, or cope, you know, and I was like—"yes! Stick it to you!"

Fatphobia as Fat Shaming and Bullying

Finally, fatphobia manifests in overt instances of fat shaming and bullying by maternity caregivers. By fat shaming and bullying, we mean language, actions, or practices, whether conscious or unconscious, that humiliate and intimidate someone judged to be fat or overweight. These practices range from a more subtle sense of annoyance and hostility from staff to name calling, physically rough handling, and intimidation. Many participants described experiences of gruffness or perceived annoyance from maternity caregivers especially when extra assistance was required because of their weight. Maia recounted her experience on the postnatal ward after her Caesarean:

They never gave me a shower. I had to get my family to shower me, even though they knew I couldn't walk. I had to have two people holding me in the shower so I didn't fall over but yeah they wouldn't do anything. They basically just treated me like a big inconvenience and that I was fat and deserved what I got, because what the hell was I doing having a baby in the first place?

Ultrasound scans were a particularly common site of this sort of fat shaming, and given the excitement and expectation with which many women approached ultrasound scans, these experiences proved deeply jarring. Leilani described her pregnancy ultrasound experience as follows:

When I was lying there, she told me "just lift all that up." Yeah, and to me, I was like "well, that's a part of me. You could have just said, "now lift your tummy up?" And you know I was thinking to myself, what's a good word? "Stomach," "tummy"— you know these are the kind of words I would use with my daughter, and not be like "lift all that up." And so I was lying there lifting my tummy ... I just felt really bad, and then she was just moving things around. It wasn't very nice; it just dampened the whole experience.

Other participants described name calling, intimidation, and physically rough handling. Participants' recounting of these experiences was often harrowing. Zoe described the painful consequences of the care she received during an emergency Caesarean section from the anesthetic team:

"It was just the lack of gentleness in their approach—speaking gruffly, man-handling my limbs around, and making little snide comments like "oh I'm never going to find the hips in here." And it was awful. I already felt like I'd failed, and then all of these comments about my weight, it just put me in such a negative space for me to meet my baby."

Jade described a pattern of intimidation and abuse from her midwife so detrimental that she decided further children were not an option for her:

She would always check my weight. She would always ask what I was eating. She would say you need to do this, you need to go for a walk, it's really dangerous being this weight ... but just the oddest things, the oddest times, every time I went to a consultation, she would drop things about my weight. Like she was like "come on, piggy, let's get on the weighing scales." It really felt kind of like bullying, and I knew I was lying down and taking it but I had to because I just wanted everything to be right for my baby.

A dominant theme running through participants' narratives of these overt shaming and bullying experiences was their preparedness to tolerate the intolerable for the sake of their babies. This tolerance highlights how fatphobia was parasitic to maternal responsibility, rendering it almost impossible to resist or reject without women feeling as though they were putting their babies at risk. Kahu described wanting to avoid maternity care as a result of shaming and bullying treatment but was resolved to persist because of her baby: "But generally I go [to appointments] because I want to know that he's alright. I want all the scans that I need to have, and all the tests that need to be done. So I'll overlook all the hurt, anger, shame I'm going to get just to know that my baby's alright. And that's pretty much it—no point in getting bitter and twisted about it because then my baby's the one that suffers."

Naming Fatphobia in Pursuit of Reproductive Justice

The narratives of our participants trace a topography of fatphobia throughout the maternity care experience. By topography, we mean that fatphobia does not have a single moment or expression in the maternal healthcare context; rather, it constitutes a terrain of interpersonal and physical, overt and subtle, encounters leading to the systemic oppression of fatness. The toll of the fatphobic encounters described by our participants on their pregnancies was a dangerous undermining of self-worth and precipitating of anxious concern for their babies. This in turn lead to a generalized loss of enjoyment in their pregnancies and compromised health. Compromised health resulted from avoidance of (or the desire to avoid) maternity care as well as mental and emotional distress, including anxiety and depression, which often leads to social isolation and, in some cases, eating difficulties. Tui described the overwhelming feelings brought on by fatphobic encounters intersecting with the other pressures she was facing while pregnant, leading to a sense of bodily dispossession:

> It was everything at once. You've got all of these [hormonal] imbalances in your body, and you're trying to deal with this, and then you've got, of course, your past body image issues, and then all of this information of what's going to happen because of my choices and my body, and so everything together. And then you just want to stay inside, you don't want to go out there, and you don't want to do what the doctor said. You don't want to go out and walk or anything. You just stay inside, and mainly eat comfort food because that's what's, you know, that's the kind of emotion that's triggered.

The irony is that medical efforts addressing the purported health risks of maternal fatness—by inadvertently or intentionally perpetuating fatphobia—actually function as a health risk in their own right.

But fatphobia is not just an issue of health gains or losses. The topography of fatphobia traced here points to the systemic oppression of fatness in the context of reproduction, which also makes it a reproductive justice issue. Reproductive justice, first articulated by women of colour and Indigenous women, offers a model for understanding reproductive health that disrupts the ideas of individual choice and responsibility, and that emphasizes the structural inequalities affecting women's reproductive health and their ability to control their reproductive lives (Price 43). Seen through the lens of reproductive justice, fatphobia is a structural oppression that produces inequalities between fat and nonfat, undermines fat women's ability to control their reproductive destinies in the face of powerful and naturalized medicalizing forces, and facilitates individualized maternal blame and sanction in place of care and kindness in maternity care encounters. However, reproductive justice also casts an intersectional lens on fatphobia focusing attention on the "links between oppressions that affect women" (Luna 358). This demands awareness to the fact that fatphobia in maternity care does not act alone nor does it affect all fat people similarly. Fatphobia intersects with, and is parasitic to, other oppressive and marginalizing forces in maternity care including racism, classism, ableism, cissexism, and heterosexism, with compounding effects for women/people whose identities are formed at these "othered" intersections.

Regardless of race, class, ability, size, gender identity, or sexual orientation, the quality of care that pregnant people receive during their childbirth journeys matters. It matters because childbirth represents a profound physical, emotional, mental, and spiritual transition in the lives of birth givers, the legacy of which is deeply felt and long lasting. The quality of care received also matters because, as childbirth advocate Sheila Kitzinger has observed, the treatment of mothers and babies during birth holds a mirror up to our culture and society demanding reflection not only on what we value, but also on our very humanity. The narratives of fat pregnant people and new mothers presented here have exposed fatphobia in maternity care as undermining human care toward both self and other with far reaching consequences. It is by naming and then addressing fatphobia along with other intersecting systemic oppressions that we can begin to secure the quality of maternity care that will support women to move forward into their parenting journeys with self-determination and positivity, while also helping to recover care as our cultural foundation. As Jade suggested, "It could actually be that big mothers are treated as people and they are helped and cared for just like how you would anyone else."

Endnotes

1 We have used the terms "woman" and "mother" in our article for ease of reference; however, we do acknowledge that not all pregnant people and new natal parents identify with these gendered terms. We also acknowledge that not all women have uteruses and that sexual and reproductive anatomy is in no way defining of gender.

2 New Zealand's largest and most ethnically diverse city of four million.

3 Names have been changed.

4 Māori are Indigenous (tangata whenua) to Aotearoa New Zealand.

5 Pasifika people are Indigenous to further islands of Te Moana Nui a Kiwa (The Great Ocean of Kiwa—The Pacific Ocean).

Works Cited

Denison, Fiona C., and Carolyn Chiswick. "Improving Pregnancy Outcome in Obese Women." *Proceedings of the Nutrition Society*, vol. 70, no. 4, 2011, pp. 457-64.

Frid, Ingvar, et al. "On the Use of Narratives in Nursing Research." *Journal of Advanced Nursing*, vol. 32, no. 3, 2000, pp. 695-703.

Gluckman, P. D., and M. A. Hanson. "Developmental and Epigenetic Pathways to "Obesity": An Evolutionary-Developmental Perspective." *International Journal of Obesity*, vol. 32, 2008, pp. S62-S71.

Heslehurst, Nicola. "Symposium I: Consequences of 'Obesity' and 'Overweight' during Pregnancy Identifying 'At Risk' Women and the Impact of Maternal 'Obesity' on National Health Service Maternity Services." *Proc Nutr Soc*, vol. 70, no. 4, 2011, pp. 439-49.

Kitzinger, Sheila. *Women as Mothers*. Random House, 1978.

Luna, Zakiya. "From Rights to Justice: Women of Colour Changing the Face of US Reproductive Rights Organizing." *Societies without Borders*, vol. 4, no. 3, 2009, pp. 343-65.

Parker, George. "Mothers at Large: Responsibilizing the Pregnant Self for the 'Obesity' Epidemic." *Fat Studies*, vol. 3, no. 2, 2014, pp. 101-18.

Pausé, Cat. "Die Another Day: The Obstacles Facing Fat People in Accessing Quality Healthcare." *Narrative Inquiry in Bioethics*, vol. 4, no. 2, 2014, pp. 135-41.

Phelan, Sean M., et al. "Impact of Weight Bias and Stigma on Quality of Care and Outcomes for Patients with 'Obesity.'" *Obesity Reviews*, vol. 16, no. 4, 2015, pp. 319-26.

Price, Kimala. "What is Reproductive Justice?: How Women of Colour Activists Are Redefining the Pro-Choice Paradigm." *Meridians: Feminism, Race, Transnationalism*, vol. 10, no. 2, 2010, pp. 42-65.

Puhl, Rebecca M., and Chelsea A. Heuer. "'Obesity' Stigma: Important Considerations for Public Health." *American Journal of Public Health*, vol. 100, no. 6, 2010, pp. 1019-28.

Simkin, Penny. "The Experience of Maternity in a Woman's Life." *Journal of Obstetric, Gynecologic, & Neonatal Nursing*, vol. 25, no. 3, 1996, pp. 247-52.

Sue, Derald Wing, editor. *Microaggressions and Marginality: Manifestation, Dynamics, and Impact*. John Wiley and Sons, 2010.

Bearing Emma Day

Chapter Two

Overfeeding the Floating Fetus and Future Citizen: "The War on "Obesity" and the Expansion of Fetal Rights

April Herndon

Although many scholars have used science and technology studies lenses to examine the ways fetal rights discourse and resulting polices are sometimes driven by emerging testing technologies and visual representations of the fetus, and feminist scholars have used their lenses to understand the gender dynamics at play, few scholars have looked at fetal rights through a fat studies lens. Now is the time. Historically, fetal rights discourse has been aided by representations of fetuses as free floating entities that are not part of women's bodies—such as the famous 1965 *Life* cover or the 2002 *Time* cover featuring fetuses as totally separate from women's bodies and often cited as iconic moments in fetus representation in the United States. Such images present the fetus as independent from the woman carrying the pregnancy and as having its own, sometimes competing, interests because it is imagined as a separate entity (Stormer, 42; Kukla 118). One of those competing interests has recently become the fetus's right to a certain kind of embodiment and/or freedom from disease. In recent history, the so-called war on drugs in the United States has created a panic about what would happen to a generation of fetuses born to women who used drugs (particularly crack) while pregnant, and what the fiscal cost for caring for such children would be.

As pointed out by scholars focusing on reproductive rights and race, many of these policies and legal rulings are part of the war on drugs have cleaved women's interests from those of the fetus. The policies did so in the name of sparing the resulting children and the nation the burden of a generation of damaged children, and, in doing so, they have further marginalized certain groups of women.[1] Today, the so-called war on obesity, the most recent social war, creates a similar panic, and as a result, discourses around fetal rights have begun to focus on risks of the fattening of the fetus. This has resulted in public discussions and policy recommendations that specifically target women who are fat as a threat to their fetuses and to the health of future generations.

Proponents of the war on obesity have taken up fetal rights discourse to suggest that fetuses are in danger of being unjustly fattened by their mothers. This fattening puts not only fetus's rights at risk but all of our rights at risk, because the nation will supposedly be unduly burdened by caring for the next generation of fat citizens. Thus, it is time to "fatten" the issue of fetal rights and examine current discourses and practices through a fat studies lens. In her article, "Disability Studies Gets Fat," Anna Mollow argues that "fattening" an issue is to take seriously the claim that fatness is a category through which our society is structured (199). In other words, "fattening" an issue, much like "queering" an issue, reconsiders the norms and constructs, and questions the underpinnings and core values expressed from the perspective of fatness and the lived experiences of fat people. "Fattening" reveals how the fetal rights discourse trades in fear to legitimize monitoring and controlling women's bodies—and the bodies of fat women in particular—under the guise of creating a healthier generation of Americans. These recommendations—which are part of the expansion of fetal rights through the war on obesity and in the name of health—fail to lead to better health for mothers, children, or the nation.

A Brief History of Fetal Rights in the U.S.

For my purposes here, I trace the history of fetal rights in the U.S. back to the 1973 *Roe v. Wade* decision, since part of the ruling suggests that the state may have a compelling interest in protecting the fetus once it reaches the point of viability. Specifically, this provision allows for the state to impose regulations around abortions after the first trimester of pregnancy (Roth 20). Scholars have watched the state's interest expand, however, as it becomes more broadly interpreted. In her book, *Making Women Pay*, Rachel Roth marks 1992 as another key turning point in the discussion of fetal rights. As she notes, the Supreme Court "reconsidered its decision in *Roe v. Wade* and replaced the trimester framework [of viability as a standard] with an 'undue burden' standard ... holding that the state has a profound interest in protecting fetal life throughout pregnancy, not just at the point of viability" (21). This new standard led to regulations such as twenty-four hour waiting periods and counselling sessions designed to discourage abortion—all with the belief that lives would be saved and/or improved by preventing abortions and keeping women from making what were believed to be hasty decisions about their reproductive lives. Well ahead of their time, many feminist scholars clearly saw that some could argue that the wellbeing of a fetus began before conception even occurred. For example, in her 1993 work *At Women's Expense*, Cynthia Daniels opines that she could imagine the interest of the fetus being invoked from the moment a woman became fertile (4). In terms of fatness and fetal rights, American society seems to have reached that point.

Fetal Overnutrition as a New Frontier of Fetal Rights

Currently, the war on obesity focuses a great deal on the uterine environment as the first line of defense against obesity, and it also represents a new point of expansion for fetal rights. "Fetal over-nutrition"—which is a phrase used to refer to pregnancies exposed to "excessive" mothers' diets, such as those containing too much fat or carbohydrates—rhetorically posits the fetus as having interests separate from the mother. Although the mother and fetus share the same body, the phrase focuses on the effects on the fetus as separate and worthy of its own consideration.

In the last ten years, as the concern about obesity has continued to grow, so have references to fetal overnutrition in medical literature. A PubMed search of "fetal overnutrition" reveals that in the last ten years, over 2,500 articles have been written on the subject, with just under 1,100 of those being written in the last five years.[2] The charge of fetal overnutrition—very much like the charges levelled against women for using drugs while pregnant—is framed within a desire to help women, fetuses, and future citizens. The reality, however, is quite different. The very concept of "fetal overnutrition" represents a new and troubling expansion of discussions about women's bodies, fetuses, and fatness because it does, essentially, realize Daniels's fear that women will be targeted from the moment they become fertile.

One landmark publication in the discussion of fetal rights and maternal obesity cited by Megan Warin and her co-authors is physician John Kral's 2004 article in *Pediatrics*, a top journal in the field. They assert the article argues that the best way to curb the obesity epidemic is to counsel young girls and women to change their behaviours so that they will not pass obesity along to their children. In 2012, Kral and several co-authors published another piece with a similar bent, this time in *Obesity Facts: The European Journal of Obesity*. They argued that there was an "urgent need" to "stem intergenerational transmission of obesity" by "preventing pregnancy in those already obese and severely obese (SO)" and to also "effectively treat people currently affected with SO to minimize the risks of gestational obesity and to optimize healthy outcomes for mother and offspring" (Kral et al. 255). They go on to make perhaps the most telling comparison of the piece, as Kral and his co-authors assert that "If Society [sic] is willing to prosecute drug-abusing mothers, and warn of alcohol and tobacco use during pregnancy, should we not be serious about preventing obese pregnancies?" (255; see also, Herndon). In sum, Kral and his co-authors posited that being fat while pregnant was at least socially unacceptable and at most criminal.

The piece was eventually featured on the *Shape Up America* (SUA) website, a nonprofit effort started by then current Surgeon General C. Everett Koop, and the organization remains closely tied to Michele Obama's "Let's Move!" campaign. Thus, having featured Kral's article weaves together concern for the unborn, panic over the obesity epidemic, and investment in a thin future citizenry.[3] The comparison Kral and his co-authors draw to prosecuting "drug abusing" mothers is especially apt given that many of the prosecutions of women for abusing drugs can be arguably tied to the beginning of the war on drugs. Furthermore, as with so many other wars against social issues, it was the women themselves who became targets rather than the drugs, and there were few positive results for either the women prosecuted or their fetuses and resulting offspring. Thus, the war on obesity and its newfound focus on fetal thinness begin to look similar to the war on drugs when scholars fatten the issue of fetal rights by examining the concept of fetal overnutrition and the resulting recommendations (Herndon).

New Pretenses and False Promises

Given the surge in publications about fetal overnutrition and claims such as those made by Kral and his co-authors, women's bodies continue to be under scrutiny as the vectors for passing obesity along to the smallest of citizens: fetuses. Although there are many reasons to be concerned about such an expansion of fetal rights discourse and the subsequent monitoring of women's bodies, in what follows, I highlight several of what I consider to be the most important and immediate issues demanding a fattening of this newly framed fetal rights discourse and the concept of fetal overnutrition.

First, arguments about the transmission of obesity expand "right to life" discourse into "right to a certain kind of life" discourse. As Ellen Willis notes, for many antichoice activists, the expansion to a so-called healthy life seems logical: "After all, if a fetus has a right to life, why not a right to health?" (91). Despite what seems to be the logic of such a claim, however, the truth is that no one can guarantee a fetus a particular kind of life or a lack of exposure to risk, or as Roth has put it, "a right to sound mind and body" (164). In other words, women are being held to a standard that cannot be met; there are no mechanisms for weeding out all possible influences on a fetus, especially since everything from lead paint to living at high altitudes can affect a fetus.

Second, because it is so difficult to tease out what influences matter at all or matter the most, the focus on obesity as a fetal influence warranting attention—and possibly even prosecution—establishes that some harms are acceptable while others are not. These standards are established around social values and ideals instead of around science or evidence, as shown by previous prosecutions of women during the war on drugs. Innumerable factors may affect a fetus; there is simply no mechanism for guaranteeing a specific sort of start to life. To focus on obesity alone represents a serious cherry picking of fetal influences. Reading the situation through a fat studies lens shows how the social values expressed by such cherry picking are driven by fatphobia as much as any evidence of real harm.

Third, the charge of guaranteeing a "certain kind of life" is also unequally applied to certain women. Historically, women who were prosecuted for drug use—many of whom were also women of colour—were seen as unfit mothers for subjecting their fetuses to harm through their drug use. In their examination of how this idea is applied to women prosecuted for drug use, Tricha Shivas and Sonya Charles assert that "this assumption [that drugs caused harm] is treated as medical fact despite the lack of evidence and the difficulty in establishing a direct causal connection in cases of in-utero harm" (186). As scholars now know from the generation of "crack babies," the supposed results of being exposed to crack in utero turned out to be nearly undetectable.

Yet, at the time, the prosecutions progressed based on the assumption that exposing fetuses to crack would prove harmful in the future. Thus, women were prosecuted based on exposure when, in fact, there was not provable resulting harm. As I have argued elsewhere, a look back over twenty years of follow up data on that generation of babies reveals that there was only a "small increase in learning difficulties ... but scientists have had a difficult time teasing out the influence of being exposed to crack from the influence of factors such as living in poverty or under stress" (Herndon 44). Similarly, the focus on harm to a fetus because of a woman's diet or weight also hinges on an assumption that there will be future harm. Furthermore, research also suggests that living in poverty and under constant stress can also influence body weight.[4] In short, it is likely as impossible to tease out why a resulting child may end up heavy as it is to tease out the influence of drug exposure in utero.

Such calls to end childhood obesity by regulating women's bodies also establish a new standard for parental responsibility to which most people would not wish to be subjected. As Daniels points out, parents have never been compelled to donate tissues, organs, or even blood to save a child's life (137), yet advocates of fetal rights now suggest that women's bodies and lives should be given over in the service of the fetus and a higher public interest. Kral's call to prosecute obese pregnant mothers and the insistence that women monitor their weight from the moment they become fertile asks for a donation of the whole body for the whole of their reproductive lives. Ironically, when it comes to obesity, members of the medical community writing about fetal overnutrition and fetal rights advocates are now sharing territory, with doctors now arguing that—at the onset of menses—young women should be counseled to keep their body weight within the defined medical range of normal so that they do not risk passing fatness along to their fetuses. This argument is not so dissimilar from fetal rights advocates who often represent women as mere containers for fetuses. Many other doctors continue to argue that women gain almost no weight during pregnancy now or even lose weight during gestation. Under such a framework, from the very moment that a woman is born, her body and life are sacrificed for the sake of future generations' thinness.

It is also worthwhile to consider what it means to place such claims alongside the power of the state, as represented by such campaigns as Michele Obama's "Let's Move!" As I explained earlier, the state has often intervened into fetal rights when it had an interest in a future citizen. The current expansion, however, seems to go beyond an interest in the citizen and into an interest in protecting the state's finances. For example, the "Let's Move!" campaign features claims about finances front and centre: "The physical and emotional health of an entire generation and the economic health and security of our nation is at stake" ("Learn the Facts"). Although people's health is often given as the reason to end the obesity epidemic, the more prominent claims are about the fiscal costs of obesity to the healthcare system and nation. Pairing the idea of a threat to our nation's security with an article such as Kral's— which suggests counselling women about their reproductive choices and perhaps even punishing women for passing along obesity— arguably expands fetal rights and further sets the stage for women's bodies to be taken over in the public interest, specifically the financial one.

Whereas something like drug prosecutions could be argued as only focusing on particular women, the expansion of fetal rights in the war on obesity puts all women at risk of interventions by intervening preconception and even premenarche. If the majority of Americans are now overweight and more than half are obese—and considering that the majority of women will give birth during their lifetimes—many women will be directly affected by the expansion of this kind of fetal rights discourse during their pregnancies. As Roth notes, about 90 percent of women give birth, which means these medical policies and discussions stand to affect the majority of women (91). Furthermore, if women must guard against eating too much throughout their lives—regardless of weight—because of their very potential to become pregnant and the assumption that "woman" and "mother" are nearly interchangeable in American society, then this means all women are at risk, as such policies expand in the war on obesity. As Karen Zivi argues, this kind of "maternal ideology" means that women's bodies become "inextricable from public health and rights arguments" (349).

Finally, such policy recommendations are largely born out of the new science of epigenetics, which means fetal rights around thinness could expand to affect men. Epigenetics—which is essentially the study of heritable traits or tendencies that result from certain genes being turned on or off—has highlighted men's important role in influencing offspring. Currently, men are mostly absent in discussions about fetuses and ending obesity, even though scholars in epigenetics have at least acknowledged that where obesity is concerned, men's diets and body weights can be just as influential—if not more influential—on a fetus. Writing about the Överkalix study, perhaps the landmark epigenetics study, a *New York Times* reporter summarized its findings this way: "What a man needs to know is that his life experience leaves biological traces on his children. Even more astonishingly, those children may pass those traces along to their children" (Shulevitz). The Överkalix study concluded that men are more influential on a fetus's development. Thus, there is potential to truly expand fetal rights discourse to every person through fetal overnutrition and the panic around the obesity epidemic, including men—a group heretofore invisible in such discussions.

Fattening a discussion of fetal rights, and their expansion, during the war on obesity takes these consequences into account and thinks about fetal rights from not only the perspective of women carrying fetuses but the perspective of fat people who may eventually be at risk for monitoring, if people's bodies are only seen as the containers for future generations. Although done in the name of children and of the future, such rhetoric is dangerous and ultimately shortsighted about the kind of future that may be created if the rights of contemporary citizens to their own bodies are undermined in the name of producing a thinner and healthier society.

Endnotes

1   I'm grateful to work by scholars such as Dorothy Roberts whose work on the assault on the reproductive rights of women of colour during the war on drugs has proven invaluable in my work. Her 1991 article, "Punishing Drug Addicts Who Have Babies: Women of Color, Equality, and the Right of Privacy," is germinal.

2   This number is taken from a search I conducted on PubMed at the Winona State University library on 13 September 2016. Using the keyword phrase "fetal overnutrition," my search yielded 2,554 articles, with 1,042 of those articles written in the last five years alone.

3   The website for *Shape Up, America!* featured the article in 2014 when I was completing research for my book. The website has since changed, but the ties to the government and nation made here are still salient.

4   The studies are almost too numerous to name here. Any search of a database such as PubMed will turn up a host of studies in which medical professionals agree that living under stressful conditions, such as those presented by poverty, can increase weight.

Works Cited

Daniels, Cynthia R. *At Women's Expense: State Power and the Politics of Fetal Rights.* Harvard University Press, 1993.

Herndon, April Michelle. *Fat Blame: How the War on Obesity Victimizes Women and Children.* University Press of Kansas, 2014.

Kral, John G. "Preventing and Treating Obesity in Girls and Young Women to Curb The Epidemic." *Obesity Research* 12.10 (2004): 1539-1546.

Kral, John G., et al. "Severe Obesity: The Neglected Epidemic." *European Journal of Obesity*, vol. 5, no. 2, 2012, pp. 254-69.

Kukla, Rebecca. *Mass Hysteria: Medicine, Culture, and Mother's Bodies.* Rowman & Littlefield, 2005.

Mollow, Anna. "Disability Studies Gets Fat." *Hypatia*, vol. 30, no. 1, 2015, pp. 199-216.

Roth, Rachel. *Making Women Pay: The Hidden Costs of Fetal Rights.* Cornell University Press, 2000.

Shivas, Tricha and Sonya Charles. "Behind Bars or Up on a Pedestal: Motherhood and Fetal Harm." *Women and Children First: Feminism, Rhetoric, and Public Policy*, edited by Sharon M. Meagher and Patrice Diquinzio, State University Press of New York, 2005, pp. 183-201.

Shroedel, Jean Reith. *Is the Fetus a Person? A Comparison of Policies Across the Fifty States.* Cornell University Press, 2000.

Shulevitz, Judith. "Why Fathers Really Matter." *New York Times Sunday Review*, 8 Sept. 2012. www.nytimes.com/2012/09/09/opinion/sunday/why-fathers-really-matter.html?pagewanted=all. Accessed 11 Aug. 2018.

Stormer, Nathan. "Embodying Normal Miracles." *Visual Rhetoric: A Reader in Communication and American Culture*, edited by Lester C. Olson et al., Sage, 2008, pp. 41-60.

Warin, Megan, et al. "Mothers as Smoking Guns." *Feminism and Psychology*, vol. 22, no. 3, 2012, pp. 376-87.

Zivi, Karen. "Contesting Motherhood in the Age of AIDS: Maternal Ideology in the Debate over Mandatory HIV Testing." *Feminist Studies*, vol. 31, no. 2, 2005, pp. 347-74.

Chapter Three

Eating for Two:
The Fear and Threat of
Fatness in Pregnancy

Megan Davidson and Sarah Lewin

Madeline[1] waited for her obstetrician to come into the exam room. Dressed only in a paper gown and socks, she sat on the edge of the padded gynecology table paging through a fashion magazine from the waiting room. Not compelled by the articles on makeup, weight loss, and the new fall trends, she was happy when her doctor knocked and entered. Before being left in the exam room, a nurse had taken her blood pressure and weighed her on the tall scale in the corner. Reviewing Madeline's chart as she entered the room, her doctor looked up from the papers and said, "You know you're not really eating for two, right?" Red faced with shame, Madeline could not reply. The doctor continued, "You have already gained too much weight for this pregnancy—thirty-eight pounds—and we have two months to go. I'm really not happy with this."

Fifteen minutes later, the appointment was over. The baby was healthy; there were no complications or concerns, and Madeline was told to come back in two weeks to be seen again. She walked two blocks and then ducked into a coffee shop and called her doula from the bathroom. "My doctor is not happy with me." She was in tears over the conversation about her weight and how her doctor had treated her.

The message that fat[2] bodies are dangerous and grotesque bombards all people, regardless of size, throughout their lives and their pregnancies. Cultural assumptions about weight and health are used to justify extensive monitoring, commenting, and managing of weight in pregnancy. Fat parents (and all pregnant people who may become fat) are shamed for endangering themselves and their future child. The fear and threat of fatness manifest as body surveillance throughout pregnancy as routine weigh-ins and concerning nutrition advice; medical care providers often provide questionable studies, imagined risks, and catastrophic outcomes.

The pressure to maintain strict weight-gain parameters is routinely cited as an incredible source of stress for clients in our NYC-based doula practices.[3] Our clients face hurtful and confusing comments, such as when Madeline's doctor said, "You know you are not really eating for two, right?" Other NYC doulas have reported witnessing nurses calling their clients "big girl"; midwives telling clients their "fat ass" was preventing them from birthing their baby; and doctors pointing to specific parts of a client's body as evidence of out-of-control weight gain. Online support groups for "plus-sized pregnancy" are filled with people who have been told their fat bodies require risky medical intervention. While these experiences are by no means universal, the medical model of using body mass index (BMI)[4] as a primary determining index of health and the larger cultural context of intense fatphobia can be challenging for pregnant people with their growing, changing bodies.

The studies available about obesity in pregnancy document a list of complications that continues to grow—diabetes, preeclampsia, hypertension, infection, birth loss, inductions, epidurals, and more Caesarean births. Plus, their babies may be big (macrosomia, or weighing over four thousand grams or eight pounds thirteen ounces), experience birth defects, and later they could become obese adults with heart disease or diabetes (ACOG "Obesity"; Chu et al. 223-28; Leddy et al. 170-178; Mayo Clinic, "Pregnancy"; Sloan). Doctors and midwives routinely remind pregnant people about these risks as a fear-based weight management tool. For example, a recent client was told by her doctor that her baby was "more likely to die" because of her current weight. Similarly, another person shared a doctor's comments, saying: "I was even told that if I did get pregnant, the chance of my baby's survival was next to nothing. I was guaranteed to have every complication possible including gestational diabetes, preeclampsia and birth defects. I was even threatened that I had a very high risk of stillborn if I didn't miscarry first. All of this was said due to my weight" (Plusmommy, "I Was Even Told").

Yet a careful reading of the studies on the risks associated with obesity and weight gain in pregnancy reveals how they are riddled with methodological inconsistencies and underexamined claims; they are not well grounded in evidence. Many of the conclusions are drawn from meta-analyses of study results in which differing criteria have been used for defining "obesity" or where BMI has been used, which can be misleading (Leddy et al. 171), and the results themselves are far less conclusive than the catastrophic warnings would suggest. For example, one study on the association between obesity and stillbirth acknowledges that "the mechanisms to explain this association are not clear" (Chu et al. 223). Another study on increased rates of Caesarean births among obese pregnant people notes that the reason for this increase is "not known" (Leddy et al. 175). Some studies even acknowledge that the outcomes they are associating with obesity could likely be "explained by other factors" (Chu et al. 223), including genetics, which one study suggests may account for as much as 90 percent of the differences being attributed to obesity (O'Reilly and Reynolds 14). The fixation on body size and weight gain as a site of risk, complications, and interventions has prevented researchers from really looking into which causal relationships may more usefully point toward having healthier pregnancies and babies.

Fatphobia and public health discourses on obesity have contributed to the ongoing moral panic about fatness) permeating prenatal care (Saguy and Riley 871; Lebesco 73). Weight gain is critical for a healthy pregnancy, but one would hardly know this from the ways it is scrutinized. Weight gain is not just evidence of a person "eating for two" but of the body supporting a growing baby (with amniotic fluid, extra blood, a placenta, new breast tissue, a growing uterus, and fat stores for breastfeeding). Caregivers' casual remarks about weight gain make these fluctuations seem not only dangerous but irresponsible. This process of prenatal management becomes a reminder that the body is risky and that fat people are unreliable and untrustworthy, are endangering their baby, and are unfit to parent.

Birth is one intimate moment in a body story, but often this story has been shaped by lifelong struggles with food and weight. As doulas, we are attentive to how this history permeates the birth space for people of all sizes and how it encourages a fear-based approach to food and body throughout pregnancy. So much of the monitoring and management throughout pregnancy is not making people safer or healthier; rather, they reproduce narratives of fat as unhealthy and immoral. In what follows, we detail how some pregnant people act in opposition to the popular culture. We see the sites of resistance to the current pathologizing model of care, in which people reclaim their dangerous bodies, birth healthy babies, and step into their role as a parent, regardless of size.

Fatphobia, Body Shame, and the Medical Management of Weight in Pregnancy

Idealizations of given body types are always culturally situated. Although concepts of the perfect body are ever changing, what remains fixed is how they are naturalized, their subjectivity unquestioned. The detrimental health effects of the current slender ideal have been well documented, yet in American culture, thin bodies and pursuing weight loss continue to be celebrated, whereas fat bodies are demonized. The ideology that weight and body size can and should be controlled by each individual is ubiquitous, both in popular culture and in medicine (Lebesco 156). Eating and exercise behaviours that would be treated as a serious health threat for one person (limited calorie intake, counting calories, and obsessive thoughts about weight or weight loss) are prescribed to others. Although there have been shifts in how thinness and health are pursued, the basic assumption that health is, and should be, achieved through thinness remains well lodged in the collective understanding of bodies.

Despite a cultural shift in language from traditional diets to a focus on lifestyle change or wellness, weight loss continues to be prescribed through food and exercise modifications, strict weight monitoring, and risky surgeries with life threatening side effects (Bacon and Aphramor 5; Lyons). Many studies have shown that the long-term health of the individual is not improved through these measures. According to Linda Bacon, chronic dieting is correlated with adverse health effects—such as hypertension, hormonal dysregulation, disordered eating, reduced metabolic rate, and decreased self-esteem, among others (49). Similarly, bariatric surgery might may successfully cause weight loss but also nutritional deficiencies and malnutrition, bowel obstruction, dumping syndrome, and poor body image (Mayo Clinic, "Gastric"). Clearly, health is more complicated than weight or BMI alone.

Both pregnant people and medical care providers approach weight gain in pregnancy through the lens of our fatphobic culture. Even though weight gain is normal and expected during pregnancy, these changes can cause distress, encourage anxiety, and create fear around food intake and exercise. Routine prenatal care is valuable, but weight management in these visits is more cultural than medical, and can act in direct opposition to the goal of health in pregnancy (Lewin 42). Weight checks, prescriptions for low fat/sugar/carb diets, lists of restricted foods, and limitations on weight gain throughout the pregnancy are all routine components of prenatal care.[5] Pregnant people are also subject to a continuous medical and social commentary on the size of their bump and baby. This weight monitoring and management can act as a reminder that the body is risky and the baby is being endangered.

Casual remarks about weight gain from care providers make these changes seem not only dangerous but irresponsible. Statements such as "you've gained more weight than I like to see," "try not to gain any more weight going forward," "limit all carbs," or "no more ice cream" are made without evidence or explanation. This advice is not grounded in research but often mirrors fad diet trends. Many of our clients assert that they are making healthful choices, despite gaining the weight their care providers expressed concern about. This aspect of their routine care is an enormous source of stress, which makes the lack of documented benefits even more concerning.

Closely monitoring maternal weight gain happens alongside the close monitoring of the fetus's size. Anxieties around "big babies" have reached new levels; according to Roni Rabin and Eugene Declercq et al., four out of five people who are warned they may be having a big baby (over four thousand grams) give birth to babies who are not big. Although the clinical recommendation is that suspicion of a big baby is not an indication for an induction or a Caesarean birth (ACOG and SMFM 13), pregnant people continue to be strongly cautioned on the risks of a big baby and encouraged (or bullied) to move forward with induction or a Caesarean birth. This surveillance of baby size is not supported by research and again highlights the cultural panic around weight and fatness above actual health.

The focus on weight as the index of health silences conversations between care provider and patient around food, movement habits, emotional health, and self-care. Harriet Brown, a journalist who has written extensively about weight and body shaming, writes that fat people routinely avoid medical care because they do not want to be shamed for their size and shape and believe, rightfully, that size discrimination will impact the quality of their care ("When Your Doctor"). Furthermore, fat people are frequently excluded from reproductive healthcare in the form of arbitrary weight restrictions limiting access to fertility and IVF treatments. Fat people seeking fertility treatments are told to return only if they radically transform their bodies (by losing half their body weight or more in some cases); they are told that otherwise parenthood is not an option for them. Size bias disables better research by circumscribing the questions researchers are asking. Additionally, it affects the quality of care offered and who is granted access to it.

Currently, pregnant people are being advised about risks that may be as much caused by the bias against fat people as by fatness itself. For example, inductions and Caesarean births are much more common for larger people and at a rate that health-related complications do not justify. This is not simply an artifact of being unhealthy or fat (Viraday, "Induction's"). Care providers bring bias to their care. In online forums for plus-sized parents, pregnant people casually talk about scheduled inductions and Caesareans for their suspected big babies, a practice not supported by medical evidence. Our clients struggle to be considered for vaginal births after Caesarean births (VBAC) because their size makes them not a good candidate. One NYC doctor described her prenatal conversations about weight gain with clients as a "golden opportunity" to improve nutrition because she views weight gain as an "objective sign" that nutrition needs adjusting. It is ironic, and sad, that the scale is understood to be objective when the entire notion that weight gain is a sign of poor health is itself not well grounded in facts. Pregnancy, regardless of size, is a "golden opportunity" to discuss nutrition and self-care, and to (re)imagine how prenatal care could adapt to increase the health of all people.

Maternal Resistance and Sites of Opposition

Long before becoming pregnant with her first baby, Natasha struggled with disordered eating and felt intense pressure to maintain her thin figure. She began binging, purging, and starving in high school, and these habits grew worse in college. With the help of a therapist and nutritionist, Natasha was able to find balance, create healthier eating habits, and forge an uneasy alliance with her body. She worried that becoming pregnant and the weight fluctuations to come could be stressful, but she felt excited about her pregnancy.

A friend recommended her obstetrician; she'd felt well cared for and happy about her birth experience. Natasha trusted the recommendation and went to her first appointment at eight-weeks pregnant. She was weighed but chose to look away from the numbers. It had been nearly a decade since she'd last stepped on a scale and seen numbers associated with her body. At the second appointment, the doctor again had her step on the scale, but this time, she commented that Natasha had gained four pounds in four weeks and should probably "slow down" or she'd end up "unhappy about the extra weight after the baby was born." Natasha was bothered by the comment but tried to set it aside and continue focusing on her changing body as a sign of a healthy pregnancy.

The next appointment was worse. "Whatever you are eating, it's too much!" the doctor exclaimed with a smile on her face. Natasha left the appointment upset. At her twenty-week anatomy scan, both she and the baby were perfectly healthy, and she was thrilled. Bolstered by the good report, she decided to speak with her doctor in hopes of curbing the doctor's comments and having less stressful appointments. With tears running down her face, she shared her history of disordered eating and explained how triggering comments about weight gain were. She assured the doctor she was eating well, working out often, and feeling healthy. She asked if they could stop talking about her weight during visits. Her doctor offered no sympathy or understanding: "I have to monitor your weight and talk with you about it, even if it makes you cry. It would be irresponsible of me not to." She then stated her continued concern with Natasha's weight and noted she was "on course" to gain forty pounds during the pregnancy.

Natasha knew that her doctor's treatment was not how her prenatal care had to be. She knew she could find another care provider who would be more thoughtful and measured in their approach. Her doula suggested practices that were less rigid and narrowly focused on weight gain as a primary measure of health. After Natasha switched doctors, she asked her doula if she should let the previous practice know why she had left their care. Her doula said, "Yes, absolutely. If they know they are losing patients over their behaviour, they might eventually change."

As doulas, we see firsthand how people both cope with and resist the current model of prenatal weight management. Labour doulas are uniquely positioned to support people who experience cultural objectification and alienation from their body and to make space for a shift in how they relate to food and weight (Lewin 49). Natasha's story of being chastised for her weight gain is common, and doulas are frequently the sounding board for people processing these interactions with care providers. Her decision to seek out alternate care, however, is a form of opposition to the current surveillance of the pregnant body. By discussing her care with her doctor and having her doula encourage her instincts to switch practices, Natasha was able to exercise authority over her body and advocate for herself and her baby.

Doulas can help contextualize the aggressive culture toward weight and bodies; they connect clients with body-positive communities, highlight faulty and inconclusive research, and affirm that they are the experts of their bodies. This approach can help clients create an alternative narrative to the one that pathologizes their bodies. For example, after her appointment at thirty-four weeks, one of our clients, Rachel, emailed an update that her baby was doing great, but her midwife was concerned about her weight gain. "She recommended I cut out all sugars and limit carbs if I want to be in the birth centre." Rachel was surprised and confused. She did not want to jeopardize the health of the baby or her access to the birth centre, but she also knew she was walking regularly and eating a balanced diet. We were able to validate her feelings, highlight the lack of evidence regarding weight guidelines in pregnancy, and contextualize comments around weight gain within a culture that sees health and weight as synonymous. We drew on our experience supporting people at all sizes to have healthy pregnancies and births. Most importantly, we reminded Rachel that "it's totally ok to assert your own boundaries around this and tell them you feel healthy and good and you'd rather they not say these things because it makes you feel bad." Rachel felt tremendous relief. Our affirming words put Rachel at ease and reminded her of all the positive things she was doing for herself and her baby. Rachel wrote "I'll re-read this whenever I feel shaky!"

Pregnancy is a time when people are particularly vulnerable targets of unsolicited advice and public scrutiny. The constant reminder that you, and your body, may harm your baby is echoed by doctors, friends and family, and even strangers on the street. This imagined risk can be silencing to people who suspect the feedback they receive around weight is an obstacle to pursuing a healthy pregnancy. Yet pregnant people can create a powerful collective consumer voice that can inspire changes to current routine weight protocols through discussing how weight is (or is not) managed during pregnancy. Though difficult, requesting your care provider not weigh you at every visit and/or keep discussion of weight to a minimum is an opportunity to advocate for yourself and assess if your provider is a good fit for you. Like previous changes within prenatal care, strong and outspoken people, like Natasha, are often at the centre of these shifts to more ethical and evidence-based care. Labour doulas have insight into a variety of practices and birth settings, which makes them uniquely positioned to affirm a client's instincts around the type of care they seek and to support them in providing alternative resources and emotional support.

In addition to the ways labour doulas and birth workers have the potential to challenge fatphobia in prenatal care on a micro level, there are nascent reclamation projects among people of all sizes sharing honest images of their pregnant and postpartum bodies on social media. Facebook groups, Instagram accounts, Internet-based projects, and hashtags (such as #plussizepregnancy and #takebackpostpartum) offer spaces to celebrate birthing bodies that do not conform to the airbrushed examples of idealized thinness offered in pregnancy magazines and advertisements. Saggy bellies, stretch marks, leaking breasts, scars, and soft curves are showcased, often alongside their own body stories. These images and stories are met with hundreds, sometimes thousands, of people praising both the honesty and bravery of the storyteller and the beauty of their exposed body. The availability of images of diverse pregnant and postpartum bodies opposes the presumption that parenthood comes in one body type and that all other bodies are less than the dictated ideal.

Not only does social media celebrate body diversity and honestly portray birthing bodies, it is a platform for fat people to document and showcase healthy pregnancies and healthy babies, and to resist the dominant cultural and medical narratives of their bodies as dangerous and diseased. For example, Tess Holliday, a plus-sized model who recently gave birth to her second child, Instagrammed a selfie of her naked pregnant body with the text "I will continue to live unapologetically, to thrive in this body, prove the naysayers wrong & laugh at the ignorance" (Mazziotta). Another fat mom-to-be posted an Instagram of herself on the beach with the text "I haven't loved every minute of my pregnancy. I've spent so many minutes crying over how my body isn't the 'normal' pregnant body ... But how lucky am I that God chose me to be a mother to this sweet little boy whom I've housed inside of my not so typical pregnant belly for the last eight months" (Peters, "If I'm Being Honest..."). Another person Instagrammed a picture with the text "This body, a body I had believed was broken, grew and birthed the most amazing little boy.... The birth of my son changed how I view my body forever!!!" (Plusmommy, "This Body"). Finally, a woman with her six-month-old son posted "I don't even notice the parts of me I don't like anymore, I just see mine and my son's happy faces." She noted that she may "always struggle" with some parts of her body but was thrilled that motherhood could "change the way you see yourself forever" (Plusmommy, "I Was Even Told"). These are powerful examples of people rewriting narratives of fatness and parenthood. Social media can be an important site for people to challenge cultural and moral assumptions about which bodies should reproduce. These images boldly affirm the health and strength of fat-birthing bodies.

Through these platforms, fat people can share stories and resources for advocacy and education as well as trade tips on size-friendly care providers and other new-parent questions. It also provides needed communities with support and encourages people who may doubt their ability to have a healthy pregnancy. These stories and experiences resist narratives of the fat body as broken. They encourage parents-to-be to trust their strong, healthy bodies and babies. This collective encouragement and body affirmation can help people to not succumb to fear-based decisions regarding their care. In this way, social media provides a unique outlet for people to heal from how they were treated during their pregnancies and in their births.

(Re)Imagining Prenatal Care

Birth is often a powerful, life-changing experience. With respectful and health-affirming care, pregnancy and birth can be a transformative site for rewriting, renegotiating, and reclaiming our bodies. For many people, this is a unique opportunity to experience their body in a positive and affirming way. In a culture where we are bombarded with messages that our bodies are not good enough, people of all sizes birthing healthy babies on their own terms, identifying their voice, and asserting their needs and desires can be profoundly healing.

There are increasing numbers of fat pregnant people in the U.S. (Putnam). There are also increasing numbers of people of all sizes who come to pregnancy with a history of disordered eating, dieting, and body hatred. We need a paradigm shift in how weight is discussed, managed, and treated in prenatal care. Data on prenatal weight gain and obesity is riddled with holes, questions, and assumptions unsupported by evidence. The current guidelines for monitoring and managing weight in pregnancy are not making people healthier. Given the maternal healthcare crisis in the US (Amnesty 1-7), doctors cannot afford to continue focusing on models for prenatal care that are not improving the health of parents and babies. It is imperative to move away from focusing on an exclusive model of health that problematizes pregnant bodies and toward bettering the prenatal care offered to people of all sizes.

We—labour doulas, birth workers, and parents of all sizes—need to demand a shift to a weight-neutral approach in prenatal care. Since the 1970s, parents have fought for radical reforms to the medicalization of birth through consumer demand: conscious birthing without general anesthesia, partners in the birth room as labour support (Wertz and Wertz 179), and, most recently, advocating for skin-to-skin contact with the baby and delayed cord clamping. Even when the evidence supported these practices, it was patient demand—not data—that ultimately made them common practices. With prenatal weight management, many care providers are clinging to faulty data and non-evidence based guidelines, but others have started to shift. One New York City doctor told us he no longer spoke with his clients about their weight gain; he preferred instead to only address health concerns if they arose. His patients had been so stressed by discussions of weight gain, and seemingly without benefit, that he changed his approach; he found his clients were no less healthy but far happier. We need to encourage more care providers to reevaluate how weight is managed throughout their care.

To support this shift, there needs to be more training opportunities available for birth workers (OBGYN's, midwives, nurses, childbirth educators, lactation consultants, and labour doulas) on how to adopt a weight-neutral framework. Instead of relying on BMI, scales, and questionable data, doctors and midwives would do better to ask their clients the following questions. How are you feeling? How are you feeding yourself? Are you eating when you are hungry and stopping when you are full? Are you eating nutrient-dense foods? Are you getting enough protein in your diet and eating ample amounts of vegetables? Are you finding ways to continue moving and getting regular physical activity? Do you feel good physically, emotionally? These questions give care providers opportunities to have meaningful conversations with their patients about health and wellness, and the importance of self-care during pregnancy. Furthermore, they provide an important space for pregnant people to practise a new way of thinking about and caring for their body. The impacts of this shift extend well beyond the months of pregnancy, and they have the potential to set the foundation for raising children who similarly have healthy and grounded relationships to food and body.

Fat people give birth to healthy babies every single day in this country, and many more could with appropriate care (Viraday, "Reply"). Thinner people frequently become fat during their pregnancies and also birth healthy babies. We do not deny that people of all sizes can face significant health risks during pregnancy and that prenatal care is necessary. That said, no amount of moralizing, shaming, and bullying is going to significantly change these realities, nor will it lead to improved health outcomes for pregnant people or their babies. We need to shift our care models in acknowledgment of this. We can and must (re)imagine prenatal care as a compassionate and evidence-based process in which people are supported and affirmed in having the healthiest pregnancies possible and are prepared to become confident parents of all sizes.

Endnotes

1   We have changed our client's names in retelling their stories.

2   We use the term fat—rather than clinical terms like "obese" or "overweight"—following fat activists who have reclaimed this term and are using it in the fight to end size discrimination and contest medical definitions of fat bodies as always sites of ill health. Fatness is culturally situated, often politically motivated, and always historically and geographically varied, so we make no claim to one definition of what a fat body is. In fact, we object to such definitions as too narrow an understanding of the embodied experience of health and wellness (as well as the entanglements of size in notions of desire, morality, and worthiness).

3   A doula is a trained birth-support person who provides continuous physical, emotional, and information support throughout pregnancy, labour and birth, and the postpartum period. Doulas are nonmedical professionals who "seek to reduce fear and build confidence, increase knowledge and informed decision-making, [and] offer practical support" and who "help preserve the memories of the birth" as a positive experience (Davidson 29). Studies have repeatedly affirmed that both mothers and babies are healthier with the support of doulas (17-18). We have both worked as doulas for many years. Davidson has been practising for over a decade and has worked with over one thousand clients. Lewin has been practising for five years and has attended over one hundred births. We acknowledge that our clients are not a fair representations of all pregnant people, as doula-assisted births only account for a small fraction of all births. Our clients all live in NYC and have the financial means to hire a doula. That said, our extensive reading of birth stories from people across the country does suggest that the stress of weight management is common across socioeconomic and geographic boundaries. Pregnant people without access to a doula—or who have hired a doula who is equally concerned with weight gain—may fare even worse.

4   BMI is a diagnostic tool for assessing health. It is the calculation of an individual's weight divided by their height, squared. This diagnostic tool has been used for assessing if an individual is underweight, healthy weight, overweight, or obese. It is a poor indicator of an individual's health.

5   The Institute of Medicine (IOM) issued weight guidelines outlining appropriate weight gain during pregnancy. Weight gain is based on prepregnancy weight and BMI, and divided into underweight, normal weight, overweight, and obese. Recommended weight gain ranges from forty pounds as the upper limit for underweight women and eleven pounds as the lower limit for obese women. (IOM). Given that the weight of the baby, the placenta, uterine and breast tissue growth, extra blood volume, and other weight gain associated with a healthy pregnancy are significantly higher than eleven pounds, this recommendation becomes a prescription to diet during pregnancy (which is agreed to be unhealthy). These recommendations are routine components to prenatal care; however, there is no research showing these guidelines improve maternal and fetal health outcomes, and there is reason to question whether they make some people even less healthy.

Works Cited

ACOG. "Obesity and Pregnancy." *The American College of Obstetricians and Gynecologists*, April 2016, www.acog.org/Patients/FAQs/Obesity-and-Pregnancy. Accessed 11 Aug. 2018.

ACOG and SMFM. "Obstetric Care Consensus 1: Safe Prevention of the Primary Cesarean Delivery." *American Journal of Obstetrics and Gynecology*, 2014, www.acog.org/About-ACOG/News-Room/News-Releases/2014/Nations-Ob-Gyns-Take-Aim-at-Preventing-Cesareans. Accessed 11 Aug. 2018.

Amnesty International. "Deadly Delivery: The Maternal Health Care Crisis in the USA." Amnesty International Publications, 2010.

Bacon, Linda. *Health At Every Size: The Surprising Truth About Your Weight.* BenBella Books Inc, 2008.

Bacon, Linda and Lucy Aphramor. "Weight Science: Evaluating the Evidence for a Paradigm Shift." *Nutrition Journal*, vol. 10, no. 9, 2011, pp. 1-13.

Brown, Harriet. "When Your Doctor Makes You Feel Fat." *Prevention Magazine*. 3 Nov. 2011, www.prevention.com/life/a20459365/weight-and-obesity-discrimination-from-doctors/. Accessed 11 Aug. 2018.

Chu, Susan Y., et al. "Maternal "Obesity" and Risk of Stillbirth: A Meta Analysis." *American Journal of Obstetrics and Gynecology*, vol. 197, no. 3, 2008, pp. 223-28.

Davidson, Megan. "Experts in Birth: How Doulas Improve Outcomes for Birthing Women and Their Babies." *Doulas and Intimate Labour: Boundaries, Bodies and Birth*, edited by Angela N. Castañeda and Julie Johnson Searcy. Demeter Press, 2015, pp. 15-31.

Declercq, Eugene, et al. *Listening to Mothers III: Pregnancy and Birth.* Childbirth Connection, 2013.

Institute of Medicine (IOM). "Weight Gain During Pregnancy: Reexamining the Guidelines." The National Academies Press, 2009.

LeBesco, Kathleen. "Fat Panic and the New Morality." *Against Health*, edited by Jonathan M. Metzl and Anna Kirkland, New York University Press, 2010, pp. 72-83.

Leddy, Meaghan, A., et al. "The Impact of Maternal "Obesity" on Maternal and Fetal Health." *Reviews in Obstetrics & Gynecology*, vol. 1, no. 4, 2008, pp. 170-78.

Lewin, Sarah. "A Doula for the Mother and the Self: Exploring the Intersection of Birth and Body Culture." *Doulas and Intimate Labour: Boundaries, Bodies and Birth*, edited by Angela N. Castañeda and Julie Johnson Searcy. Demeter Press, 2015, pp. 39-51.

Lyons, Pat. "Prescription for Harm: Diet Industry Influence, Public Health Policy, and the 'Obesity' Epidemic." *The Fat Studies Reader*, edited by Esther Rothblum and Sondra Solovay. NYU Press, 2009, pp. 75-87.

Mayo Clinic Staff. "Pregnancy and "Obesity": Know the Risks." *Mayo Clinic,* 27 March 2015, www.mayoclinic.org/healthy-lifestyle/pregnancy-week-by-week/in-depth/pregnancy-and-obesity/art-20044409. Accessed 11 Aug. 2018.

Mayo Clinic Staff. "Gastric Bypass Surgery, Risks. Mayo Clinic." *Mayo Clinic,* 3 Nov. 2016, www.mayoclinic.org/tests-procedures/bariatric-surgery/about/pac-20394258. Accessed 11 Aug. 2018.

Mazziotta, Julie. "Tess Holliday Has a Message for Everyone Who 'Can't Tell I'm Pregnant'." *People,* 19 May. 2016, people.com/bodies/tess-holliday-posts-nude-pregnancy-instagram/. Accessed 11 Aug. 2018.

Peters, Brittany. (Mrsgallypeters). "If I'm Being Honest..." *Instagram,* 16 Aug. 2016. www.instagram.com/p/BJMBlbKjIll/. Accessed 11 Aug. 2018.

Plusmommy. "This Body, a Body I had Believed Was Broken…" *Instagram*, 8 Sept 2016, www.instagram.com/p/BKGvqRFBT2g/?taken-by=plusmommy. Accessed 11 Aug. 2018.

Plusmommy. "I Was Even Told That If I Did Get Pregnant…" *Instagram*. 5 Oct. 2016, www.instagram.com/p/BLKS3GQBwkD/?taken-by=plusmommy. 11 Aug. 2018.

Puhl, Rebecca and Kelly Browne. "Bias, Discrimination, and "Obesity"." *Obesity Research*, vol. 9, no. 12, 2001, pp. 788- 805.

Putnam, Claire. "Pregnant, Obese… and in Danger." *New York Times*. 28 Mar. 2015, www.nytimes.com/2015/03/29/opinion/sunday/pregnant-obese-and-in-danger.html. Accessed 11 Aug. 2018.

Rabin, Roni Caryn. "When a Big Baby Isn't So Big." *New York Times*, 11 Jan. 2016, well.blogs.nytimes.com/2016/01/11/high-birth-weight-predictions-are-often-inaccurate/. Accessed 11 Aug. 2018.

Saguy, Abigail and Kevin Riley. "Weighing Both Sides: Morality, Mortality and Framing Contests over 'Obesity." *Journal of Health Politics, Policy, and Law*, vol. 30, no. 5, 2005, pp. 869-921.

Sloan, Mark. "Delivery by Cesarean Section and Risk of Obesity In Preschool Age Children; Research Review." *Science and Sensibility*, 21 June, 2012, www.scienceandsensibility.org/blog/delivery-by-cesarean-section-and-risk-of-obesity-in-preschool-age-children;-research-review. Accessed 11 Aug. 2018.

Viraday, Pamela. "Reply Turned Post: Ghettoizing Fat Pregnant Women." *Well Rounded Mama,* 2 Dec. 2009, wellroundedmama.blogspot.com/2009/12/reply-turned-post-ghettoizing-fat.html. Accessed 11 Aug. 2018.

Viraday, Pamela. "Induction's Relationship to Cesareans in High BMI Women." *Well Rounded Mama.* 15 Apr. 2015, wellroundedmama.blogspot.com/2015/04/inductions-relationship-to-cesareans-in.html. Accessed 11 Aug. 2018.

Wertz, Richard, and Dorothy Wertz. *Lying-In: A History of Childbirth in America, Expanded Edition.* Yale University Press. 1989.

Beauty in the Eye of Eternity Sid Robitaille (Sitka)

Chapter Four

Goal Weights, Planned Parenthood, and Aging Past My Prime: A Reproductive Timeline[1]

Emily R.M. Lind

Age: Thirty-three.

Scene: My father's bedside, in hospice.

My father is dying; doctors give him weeks at most. He has been sick fewer than six months, and I am learning time is impossible to predict or control. "Are there any conversations we need to have before I die?" he asks. "No," I say (lying). What more could I possibly say? Gingerly, I ask, "Are you mad I am thirty-three and haven't yet had children?" "No." he says. And smiles gently, "But it's not a terribly wise choice."

What is a feminist meditation on motherhood if it is not centred on the notion of choice? Raised as I was, in a prochoice family, I had always expected my path to motherhood would be paved with timed intentions. I would create the family I intended. I would get pregnant as soon as I decided to try. I would choose the life I would end up living. Future-me glimmered with crystal clarity as I imagined the ages at which I would begin planning my pregnancies. I was certain I wanted several children, certain I wanted to finish birthing by forty years of age. Growing up, I inherited a temporal framework for family planning infected with classed guidelines and assumptions: teenage pregnancy was something to be avoided at all costs; professionalization was a prerequisite for parenting; and a formalized relationship was the context in which children *should* be raised. To have children in any other context was simply to choose the wrong choice. To have children too young or with too few resources would be to risk my family's future. And what kind of fool would choose the wrong choice? By the age of thirty-three, I had watched the majority of my friends cross over into parenthood, and I was beginning to worry I had chosen the wrong choice.

Pregnancy and family planning are inescapably temporal endeavours. Conception is timed according to the last menstrual period, fertility rates appear married to maternal age, and respectability maxims dictate good versus bad ages at which to get pregnant. To grapple with one's self as a reproductive agent is to confront a temporal script that enlists both the body's (in)capacity for reproduction and personal intention. Similarly, fatphobia imagines fat bodies in temporal terms. Fat is often a consequential symbol of undisciplined food and exercise choices (Bordo; LeBesco). Temporally speaking, fat bodies are considered to be in states of "after"—after aberrant weight gain—as though fat bodies are not normally occurring variants of the human condition. Furthermore, fat bodies are also imagined as future-thin bodies, awaiting a transformative surgical, diet, and/or exercise intervention. In the last twenty years, critical scholars have begun theorizing the epistemological possibilities rendered through asynchronous temporalities. Crip time and queer time have emerged as conceptual tools that help expand the terms of understanding how marginalized lives are lived, and the possibilities that exist outside of measurable or anticipated temporal frameworks.

This chapter is a personal essay that reflects upon my entrance into and out of peak reproductive time and how fatphobia shaped my experience of my body as a potentially reproductive agent from the ages of eight to thirty-five. I am using queer and crip temporalities as theoretical lenses through which to consider the ways that the normative life course imposes a series of temporal expectations upon bodies and desires, which maintain raced and classed logics. Queer time as oppositional informs Lee Edelman's claim that "queerness can never define an identity; it can only ever disturb one." (17) Similarly, fat subjectivity is lived in opposition to normative temporal expectations (Lind et al)—such as age-specific weight guidelines for children, moral panics insisting fat bodies will die sooner than thin ones, and weight loss goal setting that restricts foods for time-specific diet plans. In particular, fat subjects disrupt the imagined outcomes of biopedagogical scripts—those ideas and practices that serve to regulate bodies in the interests of conforming to a healthy or normative ideal. Diet regimes, fitness tips, weight-management plans, and nutritional advice are all sites of biopedagogical instruction. The recipients of such lessons are encouraged to adopt regulating practices that, as Jan Wright argues, enable subjects to "*understand* themselves, *change* themselves and *take action* to change others and their environments" (2, emphasis in original). The presence of fat bodies exists symbolically as failed lessons in self-understanding, change, and action. Indeed, my body has often been read as a site of failure. Fat time figures motherhood differently. Or at least, my narrative takes place in fat time.

Age: Eight.

Scene: Doctor's office. Checkup, with my mother and baby brother in tow.

The doctor finishes his exam and concludes by asking my mother "are you concerned about her weight?" I brace myself for Mom's vicious retort. I am familiar with her take-no-prisoners attitude toward men in positions of authority. He gently taps his BIC pen on my thigh as he asks, "are you concerned?" "Well," she says, softening into his question, "a bit." I'm shocked. Why would she be concerned about my weight? He immediately launches into an interrogation of what she's been feeding me, and finds his culprit: apple juice in my lunch box. I'm prescribed a diet to lose weight, encouraged to set goal weights and timelines, and given diet soda in my grade-three lunchbox. I have not yet menstruated. Not yet learned long division. "What do you want your goal weight to be?" the doctor asked. I had no idea how to respond. I didn't think of myself as a particular weight—past or future. It hadn't yet occurred to me that I needed to set a goal for my future self. The year I learned how to sign my name in cursive, I was initiated into toxic lessons about how to assess the number of calories on my plate and how to question my hunger cues. I developed a piercing awareness that my eating was being watched and scrutinized.

Later, I would learn that eight-year-old girls typically gain significant weight as the body prepares for menstruation and that the body may understand fat as necessarily reproductive. The visibility of fat on my body was assumed to be the consequence of poor food choices, as opposed to normative physical development. I didn't know it at the time, but fat shaming from doctors would become a common part of my experience of medical service provision as I transitioned into adulthood. No one told me that my body was fat because I was transitioning from child to woman. No one told me that my eating was being scrutinized because women aren't trusted with their own bodies.

Early entry into diet culture had epistemological consequences: my knowledge of my body became oriented around weight. The following is a list of formalized diet plans I was either forced to follow or willingly inflicted upon myself, all before the age of sixteen: weight watchers, the Scarsdale diet, a sugar-free diet, and a carb-free diet. I was taught to weigh myself in the morning before breakfast to retrieve authentic data. I was taught that drinking water containing ice cubes burns more calories because the body uses more energy to stay warm. I learned never to eat after 7:00 p.m., never to eat more than two pieces of bread in a day, and never to exceed the prescribed ounces of poached chicken as I prepared my daily salad. These biopedagogies, ostensibly taught to promote healthy behaviour, were ultimately lessons in alienation. These lessons were delivered to generate a thin future—one where my body would be easily assimilable into standardized weight guidelines, magazine images, and beauty ideals. Diet culture perverted my sense of the present tense; it commanded me to alter my behaviours and self-perception in the interests of being thin in the future. To paraphrase from Alison Kafer's examination of crip futurity, a fat body is "a future no one wants" (2).

Despite my attempts to adopt these behaviours, with every failed diet came the secret my flesh continued to proclaim: *my body was supposed to be fat.* My body would make up for every stolen pound, every time they were lost, she'd take them back. In the medical imagination, fat is characterized as a changeable physical characteristic, implying that if one *remains* fat, that person has simply chosen to live in a fat body (Puhl and Heuer). Beyond choice or intention, weight re-gain felt as natural as breathing, an involuntary corrective to the willful shrinkage I had attempted, over and over again, to achieve. My body remained a symbol of excess despite constant attempts to shrink it. My fat body was undisciplined, feral, insubordinate.

Age: Twelve.

Scene: Laundry room.

My mother finds blood-stained underwear in the laundry bin, and approaches me with tentative excitement. "I think you've gotten your period, Em," she says. She has an adorable smile on her face that I can still see in my mind's eye. She books a reservation at a fancy restaurant for us to have a special mother-daughter meal to celebrate. At dinner, she gives me a gold-chain necklace and reads me passages from Simone de Beauvoir's The Second Sex and poems by Marge Piercey. I am proud to have gotten my period. My mother calls me a "woman." I learn that blood is sacred and something to celebrate. Three weeks later, I am instructed to inspect for stains I leave on the toilet seat when menstruating. "You must not have noticed," she says, "but you need to be more careful now that you're bleeding."

I am shocked when my period returns the next month. The grammar of anticipation had tricked me into thinking it was a one-time event: to get one's period. Now I had it. But it was all a lie. I didn't have my period; I'd be getting and getting and getting and getting and getting my period indefinitely. The first period was worthy of celebration. And the endless getting was a chore to be cleaned.

My initiation into fertility was an initiation into the disciplinary labour of regulation, correction, and measurement. Naturally, my body was a site of chaos. Unruly, immeasurable, and therefore risky, my body needed to be reined in. I had to hide its physicality, its secretions and filth. Around the same time, the public school system began educating me on my body. Zoomed-in photographs of infected genitalia were broadcast year after year as I entered senior public school and then high school. Sexuality had consequences, so the lesson went. Contaminated, disease-ridden consequences. Or worse yet: teen pregnancy. These lessons confirmed the earlier biopedagogies taught to me by doctors—my body was a site for control and regulation, and my choices were the central lens through which my body's future would be secured.

Age: Sixteen.

Scene: Math class.

I'm sitting in math class, in the middle of a math test, and I look over at the boy sitting next to me, distracted by his gestures catching the corner of my eye. I glance up, and I can tell he can't see me. He can't see me because he and another boy are mocking my body without words. They are running their hands over their body parts, tracing the phantom boundaries of where my oversized thigh would measure on their small, taut legs. One boy traces the contours of an imaginary inflated stomach; another responds by blowing up his cheeks to solicit a quiet chuckle. I am horrified and I am shocked. I don't know what to say; no one else is seeing this. I am frozen in my witnessing. But I can't stop watching, as the contours of every inch of my body is reenacted on their own, and then, once my entire body has been hyperbolically outlined, the boy next to me goes in for the punchline and outlines enormous breasts. I am suspended between flattery and shame. I can't believe they've noticed my breasts. I remain horrified, but horror isn't the only feeling running through me. I feel redeemed or at least, only part monster. I am both disgusting and sexual. And at least through their objectification, I feel sexual. Is this how sexuality will always feel? I wonder. Will I only feel sexual and feminine after first being characterized as monstrous?

Age: Seventeen.

Scene: Basement rec room.

I am watching a movie at a friend's house. She's invited Sarah and me over. My friend's older brother, who I recognize from high school hallways, walks into the room, takes one look at Sarah and me, and quips, "What's this? Beauty and the beast?" I am speechless. His quick one-liner is the confirmation I fear the most: I am monstrous, beastly. In the eyes of the boys at school, I am disgusting and aberrant. More importantly, I am an undesired counterpoint to objects of desire. I am sick with confusion over how to navigate this dynamic: girls set up as competitors for the attention of mean boys. How to proceed?

Age: Nineteen.

Scene: Outdoor restaurant patio.

My father and I are lunching with a longtime family friend. They reminisce about being undergrads at York University, and ask me if I like the campus. I say something about the underground tunnels being nicknamed "rape tunnels" and that I far prefer the University of Toronto's campus because it's integrated into the well-lit cityscape. "You shouldn't have a problem with that," my father's friend says casually, "You're hearty." I feel "caught"— exposed for fearing sexual violence when clearly I'm not the kind of body that is imagined to be at risk for rape.

These were the terms in which heterosexuality was presented to me: men as mocking, critical, and verbally abusive. Their characterization of me as monstrous was only confirmed by the clothing stores that disavowed the existence of my shape or size and by the doctors warning me that my body was dangerously large and deserved to starve. I was failing to fit at being straight, failing to fit at being girl (Rice). Not only did the pleasures of heterofemininity not fit, quite literally, neither (supposedly) did its violences. Heterosexuality was presented to me as a paradigm where love for my fat self simply did not exist. Heteronormative futurity was denied within the logic that characterized my body as beastly and unattractive. And if, as Jack Halberstam has argued, temporal normativity is marked by heterosexual benchmarks that follow a trajectory from dating to marriage to childbirth to retirement, then my future was unknown and unclear. Fatphobia contributed to my failure at heterosexual success. It also prevented me from questioning the life of my own desire. If participation in heteronormative rituals constitutes success, then fat bodies may be read as failed heterosexual subjects. Put another way: my experience of fatphobia revealed compulsory heterosexuality as an institution of violence. It attuned me to seek different ways of being in the world. Indeed, my experience of fatphobia queered me in relation to compulsory heterosexuality to the extent that I actively sought, in Halberstam's words, ways to "open up new life narratives and alternative relations to time and space" (1-2).

Age: Twenty.

Scene: Second-year university; Feminist theory class.

I fall in love with the hyperarticulate butch dyke sitting at the back of the classroom. She calls me the most beautiful woman she's ever met. We roll our eyes over the ways straight friends of ours accommodate the men in their lives; she takes me shopping in plus-size stores, and her eyes sparkle when I try on clothes. We move in together after two years of dating. I feel free from the pressures of heteronormative dating, immune from the expectation that I need to cater to the whims of male desire. I feel loved. There is room for my body here. I am not a before photograph. I am not monstrous. I am her ideal.

Age: Twenty-nine.

Scene: Conversation with my mother.

The summer I turn twenty-nine I am invited to nine weddings in twelve weeks. Every single one of them is in a different city, none of which I live in. I spend all of my disposable income on Greyhound bus tickets and travel to various country banquet halls and rural churches. I am shocked at the number of friends who wear white (note: one hundred percent), and am surprised when their fathers "give them away." A year later, the babies start coming. I ache to participate in the transition to parenthood but loathe the rite of passage that appears to herald the advent of maternal time in many of my friends' lives. I turn to my mother, as she hands me the ninth invitation of the season, and I am exasperated, tired, broke, and can't afford any more time taken from my dissertation work to attend this last wedding. "It's important to recognize the transitions in people's lives," she says, patiently. "But Mom," I groan. "Is no one else writing a book?"

Queer consciousness created a different centre from which to understand my body's currency. I have failed extravagantly at some of the heteronormative milestones the way a proud queer does. The ways I have failed at heteronormativity in many ways are also the ways I succeeded at being queer. But where is parenthood within the queer trajectory? Does parenthood have "no future" in the queer timeline, as Edelman has suggested? Certainly, same-sex couples can and do mimic heterosexual time in their quest to reproduce biologically following a state-sanctioned marriage—a sensibility some have called homonormative (Duggan; Puar). Failing at being straight had become a delight, an opportunity to escape the cacophonous insistence to conform to compulsory heterosexuality's demands (Rich). But as I approached the age of thirty, time felt as though it were accelerating. I couldn't see models of how to parent outside of heteronormative structures. I happened to be single, and while that wasn't a problem for my heart, it felt as though it were catastrophic for my hope of having children.

Age: Thirty-four.

Scene: Doctor's office, annual physical.

My doctor asks me if I want to be referred for fertility treatments, although I have not mentioned pregnancy once. "You're in your mid-thirties. And statistically, it is very difficult to get pregnant after thirty-five. There's a real cliff—you don't have the time you might think you do. If you want children, I recommend you begin planning them now."

For the first time in my life, my body's future was being read by a doctor beyond the boundaries of weight stigma. Her comments were as liberating as they were cautious. My body was being read as ready for motherhood. Reproductive time had eclipsed weight-loss time as a medical priority in a "mutual contamination of nows" (Hutchings 166-67). Being invited to consider family planning by a medical service provider gave me a taste of an "accessible future" in Kafer's terms.

By the age of thirty-four, some of my friends had begun separating from their partners; their children are now going to be raised in blended families like the ones my friends and I were raised in. The nuclear family model was once again proving difficult to sustain. All of a sudden, I was surrounded by friends entering into new relationships with their kids in tow and friends leaving relationships to single parent. I felt increasingly entitled to imagine a similar future for myself. I approached a gay friend and asked if he'd be willing to be a known donor, enabling me to conceive a pregnancy as a single mom by choice. He was game. We met for dinner once a month for two years, imagining every scenario, going over every possible outcome. At every turn, we felt closer to each other, established deeper relations of trust, and felt clear that we were choosing the family we wanted while invoking a "new way and form of living" (Ahmed 559).

Age: Thirty-five.

Scene: Downtown Toronto condo.

We have a deal. I'll bring the wine; Matthew will bring the home insemination kit. We'll split the cost of take-out. The whole exchange takes less than thirty minutes. I insert the applicator full of ejaculate into a cap that hugs my cervix for hours. Once I am inseminated, we sit on the couch, eating second helpings of pad thai and refilling our glasses. "Can you believe we're doing this?" we exclaim excitedly to each other, over and over again. "Yes and no." We keep saying. Yes and no.

What is the cost of a queer imagination? My decision to conceive a child with the help of this sacred friend leaves me feeling excited, ecstatic, and optimistic about the future. I delight in the ways this choice pushes us to use new language and invent new modes of kinship. My donor calls the fetus "sparkling" and marvels at his impending role in our child's life as a "spuncle." At the age of thirty-five, I find my nonconforming relationship choices are escaping excessive familial scrutiny due to the fact that I am pursuing parenthood before it's too late. We have been dreaming of this scenario for two years, yet there are parts of me that still cannot believe it, parts of me that are still forming the epistemological muscles required to make sense of this alternative reality. José Muñoz recognizes queerness as the "rejection of a here and now and an insistence on potentiality ... for another world" (1), and that is, I believe, precisely what is guiding Matthew and I as we enter into a relationship without role models, without a script. We are guided by our desire to reject the models we were raised with, and anticipate that by doing so, we can invoke a radical future for ourselves and my child. The teetering between knowing this is happening and having it lurk beyond belief reminds me of Muñoz's contention that queerness is not yet here: "we may never touch queerness, but we can feel it as the warm illumination of a horizon imbued with potentiality" (1). Nevertheless, he continues, "queerness is primarily about futurity and hope" (11). By rejecting the biopedagogies that would have my fat body read as diseased and inactive, I claimed a queer futurity built on hope—one located beyond the purviews of compulsory heterosexuality and one capable of sustaining my entry into motherhood in good time.

Age: Thirty-five.

Scene: Midwifery Office, monthly check-up.

I consent to letting the young midwifery student lead my monthly appointment. I am seven-months pregnant, and by now accustomed to the routines of these meetings. "Okay," the student says, "Can you lie back and let me measure your belly?" I obey, and as the tape reaches across my abdomen, she looks concerned and up at my midwife. "What's wrong?" I ask, about to panic. "It's just ... um ... okay so your measurements are off. Technically you're measuring at a later stage of pregnancy but..." she trails off. My midwife intervenes, "I've been recording Emma's measurements according to her own numbers, not the standardized scale. You'll see her numbers generate the same curve as the textbook, just measuring at a different part of the graph."

In pregnancy, the pregnant body and the fetal body are both dated by time *and* size. The bigger you and the fetus register, the more time the clinical guidelines assume you have been pregnant. The student's reaction to my body was simultaneously physical and temporal: I was measuring (size) at a later stage (time) of pregnancy. Her comment begs a deeper exploration of the potential of fat futurity. Rather than too slow, was I ahead of the curve? Are fat bodies more like microwave ovens as they bake babies, needing seemingly less time? I am, in medical discourses, considered a geriatric mother, or *of advanced maternal age*. In traditional discourses of economic success, I am risking a life of poverty by choosing to remain unwed. These discourses produce a story about my body that implies my personal history was a mistake: to avoid these labels, I *should have* gotten married earlier so that I *would have* children by now. These discourses invent a mythical narrative where not only did I *have* the choice to get married and bear children at an earlier age, but that I would necessarily have *wanted* to. Confronting the twinning of chance and desire within the logic that places me "out of time" both physically and economically pulls me back to Halberstam's claim that heteronormativity is invested in these logics. The temporal logic that labels my thirty-five year old body as "geriatric" is a logic that expected me to prioritize child-rearing in my twenties—a decade largely spent in graduate school (advancing my understanding of social power) and psychotherapy (unlearning the toxic dynamics embedded within my family of origin). Of course, as a fat woman, I am no stranger to being told my body and my choices are out of time, unfit, and undesired.

Instead, I have done this in fat time—time spent slowing down the narrative and seeing the possibilities of not keeping up, of not fitting in. Fat time happens outside the field of vision of medical authority, and I have learned to trust the wisdom that comes with waiting. My body may be labelled geriatric in maternal time, but maternity has always been a tempo imposed upon women before they had the capacity to wrestle with it. Finally outside of the timelines heteronormativity would otherwise have me follow, I find the space to claim my own maternal agency outside of the male gaze and outside of the nuclear family model. As my belly gets bigger and rounder, I delight in my growing shape as a sign and symbol of productivity and chosen labour. It has helped me cultivate an expansive sense of queer imagination.

Endnotes

1   Dedicated to Matthew J. Trafford and Christopher Ruth Gordon Lind.

Works Cited

Ahmed, Sara. "This Other and Other Others." *Economy and Society*, vol. 31, no. 4, 2002, pp. 558-72.

Bordo, Susan. *Unbearable Weight: Feminism, Western Culture, and the Body*. University of California Press, 1993.

Duggan, Lisa. "The New Homonormativity: The Sexual Politics of Neoliberalism." *Materializing Democracy: A New Cultural Politics*, edited by Russ Castronovo and Dana D. Nelson, Duke University Press, 2002.

Edelman, Lee. *No Future: Queer Theory and the Death Drive*. Duke University Press, 2004.

Halberstam, Judith. *In a Queer Time and Place: Transgender Bodies, Subcultural Lives*. New York University Press, 2005.

Hutchings, Kimberly. *Time and World Politics: Thinking the Present*. Manchester University Press, 2008.

Kafer, Alison. *Feminist, Queer, Crip*. University of Indiana Press, 2013.

LeBesco, Kathleen. *Revolting Bodies? The Struggle to Redefine Fat Identity*. University of Massechusetts Press, 2004.

Lind, Emily R.M, et al. "Reconceptualizing Temporality in and through Multi-media Storytelling: Making Time," *Through Thick and Thin. Fat Studies Journal*, vol. 7, no. 1, Forthcoming.

Muñoz, José, *Cruising Utopia: The Then and There of Queer Futurity*. New York University Press, 2009.

Puar, Jasbir. *Terrorist Assemblages: Homonationalism in Queer Times*. Duke University Press, 2007.

Puhl, R.M. and CA Heuer. "The Stigma of Obesity: A Review and Update." *Obesity (Silver Spring)* vol. 17, no. 5, 2009, pp. 941-64.

Rice, Carla. "Becoming 'The Fat Girl': Acquisition of an Unfit Identity." *Women's Studies International Forum*, vol. 30, no. 2, 2007, pp. 158-74.

Wright, Jan. "Biopower, Biopedagogies and the Obesity Epidemic." *Biopolitics and the "Obesity Epidemic": Governing Bodies*, edited by J. Wright and V. Harwood, Routledge, 2009, pp. 1-14.

Section II:
(Don't) Let Them Eat Cake:
Experiences of Fat Kids

Chapter Five

I am not Small

deborah schnitzer

       I am not
small
inside my head where I
       watch one calloused
hand whitegloved
turn up two backseamed
ankles stockinggrey
       watch another
stretch toward openbottomed thighs
shimmy scat under the five-and-dime
slip
       not small no
sitting careful on her side of the mattress
feet swinging soundless above pebbly carpets
as she prepares to leave my body
       counting parts
     one two buckle my

not small
though I shrink between her and this
fat
   her she seems to have got us
   the one
   workgone at dawn but come

back at 5:15 with lenses thick
 a
bat
  teringram
though the door opens and we trained swift
scuttle

not small no
because I
   look quiet as she reaches for the handle
   toes pointed into sidewalk pumps
   her thicker purse telling me she
   cannot stay
not small
because I
   have precious tomorrow words
   stored safety in my digging closet and
   a safety song to go with

heigh ho! heigh ho!
   if you get away
   and no one comes to bring you
   back They cannot leave you here no
    They cannot Someone has to come to save
     Someone can save

my safety where I song my head sings even when I sit
   on the bed to
  watch
my doubling mother stand quick
     make no blowing kiss but
    tsk tsk her way along the hall
    banister
     d
    own its
     seven

          stairs
                  across his living room
         through one
       screen
     door
   a stoop
the dish runs away with

my head remembers red
              lipsticking her teeth
              me sucking my cheeks
              to look
              like her
my heart remembering
that
it does not know who she is except she seems bigger
      than she wants to be
that
      when she talks
I don't want the sound she makes
 (but always I want the cookies which she bakes far from her face her
flour fingers dusting bins)

in knots
              she is returned by her father
              who says she must lie
              in a bed she made one afternoon
              just after the second world war
              where this husband our father
                  — the one she got—
              started making us up
            in her
       and wasn't that a dainty dish to set before
         in me
       in my entirety with
      a body close to the ground that cannot tie up its own hair

when she is repossessed she passes
through the canal I am become
in the stair way from stoop to foyer
with the grey suit which she would not
take off its opentoed grey suede platforms almost
trained away from

she is
naked
the look she gives
not the kiss
scoured
the chance she took
not the sink

not small no

I would not cry if all alone
(without the lap she could make on Tuesday nights
when he was sure to be gone, her lap roomy set
on the couch and we could open our mouths)

_____not have cried if unretrievable she
had set her free and
_____if years after she would have seen me coming safer
higher

but they brought her back low
and then
we cried for
we were never going any

where

I have so many
heigh-ho
songs to sing lined up
       utensils at the

midnight fridge
ice cream cartons unlacing
my holy mother wrapped in pharmaceuticals
ruined

could she **hickory dickory**
see her first-time face
more beautiful than before or after fat fixations
this woman who becomes the mother
I see in a picture from the painted bowl I keep in front of my
fireplace her Ava Gardner dimples on a man's arm
a *Clark Gable* double (that's what They say) in
some MGM Hollywood lot loving her
for They, the older women, these
auntie handlers in our family send her
away **to market to market to buy**
because there is no wedding day in the thirties
            when the around-the-corner-man
                    —our father—
            promises he would wed
        at least that is as legend has
                he asked
                forgot
                too fat
                was she
              and thus
            sent south
          for trimming
        perhaps
how now brown cow
salvageable if smaller

what would I know for certain I am
    too busy looking through
  the excuse that
    put her on the train

watercress
　　coastal
　California
thinning out the war years
　　he lost his hair
　　　some teeth
gained an aversion to lamb in training himself young men to shoot in
battles he could not to kill directly but seeing my mother after

when returned
having forgotten
saw
　　　the less of her
　　　　　took up where she was
　　　　　　　relinquishing her fedora **ding dong, bell**
they made up
too many children
too quickly **there was an old woman**
they forgot?
didn't even try?
were eating their hearts

her body took back its flesh
I made mine up out of vigilance and junk food ripple chips stuffed
under sectional seats stiff in a sodapop sticky couch stuck in cellar-
wreckroomfallout shelter in a house they bought with help my
mother's father dole

I was always chewing chips waiting for my brother late who wasstuck
to licking necks in parking lots hickey chews and burrowing he
necking but I nevernotever only chips slipped or Twizzlers, Cheezies,
Mr. Big

coming to obese naturally and with supervision

fat doctor examining fat child examining

fat child's thigh rolled out flat
on examining table fat doctor plumbed

thumb and index finger pinching fat
child's excess circumscribing crust
with red insoluble marker to help
fat child's father identify areas
fat child has made to thus
be eliminated in fat doctor's
clinic where fat child can
be sent to treadmill af-
ter-school Wednes
days and on Satur
day mornings
with fat wo-
men not ea-
ting **little**
Jack

my body beautiful
does not know she is
cannot tell **doctor fell**
my sides open shut
with fisted chips
punch to judy
my coat wrack with mistakes
cupboards burst
my mother from bed leaps into slip
joins mouthful
our bare feet lining up
like kitchen windows our
neighbour lights look at
pease porridge hot
she is so mother
we are too much

jammed corners
where is our good

dear toofat mother,

>> if we did not say
>> if we tried harder to cut

>> how could we
>> was there a way

>> what was the look on my not-so-big fat face
>> devious. carceration. comfort.

> lovingly,
> I am reminded
younger
we were
dressed in matching tea parties I am
set between my grandmother Mimi and you
at a Dr. Smith's wife's outdoor fundraiser

I am afternoon pretty
oh so navy blue
buckled shoe
pleats head cocked
sunlight squint
you are there in a
wide brim beside
Mimi's not-afraid smile
the one she had sometimes
when the spring water isn't deep
(because I think she lost someone little there
a long time ago)

Mimi is rolly polly pretty

you too

what is rolly polly pretty
what is memory
is the world round and loving learned

my goodenough fat mother's big heart
repeatedly sets me out in my most adorable outfit
saddleshoes unscuffed
checkered cuffed Capri with white button embellishment
highwaisted decorative faux pocket inserts
sailor blouse anchored by symmetrical red and white stripes
fetching blunt cut short bangs swept to right side spiffy

she loves me though
growing not small
I too am sent to thinning camp
stuffing **hush little baby**
gifts torn my crown broken down
don't you cry why not?
I open my lips, mightier than the Euphrates, overflowing, unprece-
dented, I swallow
cupboards I pray

      dear fat lady of sorrows
      cross the moons of shame

      come with your carving knife
dig into the dead of night and take my flesh as water into the throats
of elsewhere skinny Saturdaycity dancing girls hip bone hands akimbo
in leotard with coloured belt pulled tight round tidy
spoil their indentation
      come deep into dumpling flesh on bed of nail tied to
measuring tape
and caliper and kiss me kiss me thin to wasting
trim me sick into please

      me
      bodyfattrimmingcampdancingme
      todietdeathjulystraightthroughtotheendofaugust

because I bulge

if guests come and I am returned to the down stairs to say goodnight

I can show the teeth of the brush drilled into the part in my hair
I can recite
there was a little girl who had a

1. Mr. Himmel might say I am
cute
my folklore saying burst in seersucker summer pajamas he might find
a regular cat's meow

2. Mr. Himmel might say
**Pussy Cat ate the dumplings!Pussy Cat ate the dumplings!
Mamma stood by And cried, "Oh, fie!**

WHY did you eat the dumplings?"
daughter of the midas
trying to touch the hoop strung over doors she cannot reach
trying to have some thoughts
trying to dribble the golden apple
trying to see the hoop
trying not to have some thoughts
trying to be invisible but all she can do is see a fat girl in a white
leatherette jacket with brown hair stringy in a driveway with a ball
and a basket her mother cannot make a basket
she can not make the basket

my basketless mother is watching from the kitchen window and this
black thing without hair is behind me is waiting for me this black
thing is behind who shoots better and who is waiting

who is afraid

I am going to free my mother and I
give us

> a loft
> our time and space
> a hundred things we know
> our food
> a caramel flyaway dress
> one lemon and raspberry Saturday morning

robes edged in cerulean
an unstained glass and holy rivering bodies in the bath

I am going to reclaim
eyes unhurt with colour returning
inflected, seagreens glad greens seeing with tenderly
redrawn
indentations the daring
intelligence of toe openings

I am tearing down accusations

flawless my fat mother is every word she ever wanted
hydrated I am in her lap if she wants me birthed if she needs me silent
if she
must dance her own two feet a siren anointed if she desires a partner
for the wiles in
dark passages where she subsides
or rises calligraphic
she can fluctuate
run her wind
sudden
fluent
she can take anything
reconvene her swell the bit on her lip
if ever I would leave you it wouldn't be in
if she wants
her throat
her voice
caresses

if she had been unfound
we would have written each other
unforgettable

despite attempts **humpty dumpty**
she has a little head cut out against her girth
stalwart standing firm in front of pointing phobic fingers

blockade
wind beats
Heigh ho
Nobody home

my mother begged in front of kitchen windows
a cat dragged out
the little dog laughed
fiddle diddle
lighter wind can stand with her
red bathrobe petting her ankles
hair unbrushed by
broom shovel scale bent against her
her matter

daylight grassairbreathmolecules circulate
she leans toward
a Hollywood boulevard unsoiled
the music in her scales
running thick her chins

she would be imprecise
could she have been the airline ticket I would have put in her purse if I
were the queen
in the world and ours such
sport to set before

I am still not

small inside my head running away with
bigger in my calculations of mother hoods for I have braided
breathtaking
fathoms
the way out
even when locked in
she, my mother, threw her voice away without her voice to tell her
things
crude and puny cutting us into sizes

that would corrode
our great hearts
tearing us with malice and forbidden I am
tenderly I am
all verses
set down for strangers who might come with nightnight lights to
doors where notsmall children are kept for target practice, their teeth
run through their tongue necks aching stretched beyond the sticks
rammed down their

quiet quiet in the please of care for

by kindness now I have sought in my daily right to
rounder versions of might
mothering for softness and dimpled lovely

even in the folds of frighten a how to

not small
in relation
I warm the swath
my mother could have been
tender thinking
in the midst of a thousand undoings
awake and carefuller unafraid of the hammering of
stores run by less and fell
I fetch my mother's picture from the painted bowl
Reframe in **heigh ho** silver
add her
open toed
traveling her
discernment

near me in bountiful
she is the size of loving as I am
I see the moon and the moon sees me

what are little girls

in my small I could not know
I was not really a size

lined up hoping those who were straightening us out would fall down
die out They
do not

we do not
tunneling
between
breast
and
jaw

vision
little miss muff
I sit now
Lavender's blue
with dusk
without goodbyes
my body running over its moons
out of
harm's way
inside stored safety my **sings**
diddle diddle
dish to
spoon
me my
fall down and rising
nursery phenomenon
sight
my lights
lifting a way
all a queens
to horses to hither
even when we cannot
we may

proseed with
less malice
more tender
weights
redrawing
looking glasses
loves measure
true mends
with
vinegar and brown paper
stitch
in time

Love Always bathbunny

Chapter Six

Conversations with Our Mothers: Exploring Maternal Blame and the Generational Effects of Body Management

Samantha Walsh and Jen Rinaldi

Our purpose is to share our personal narratives illustrating the impact of body expectations on our respective maternal relationships. These narratives and the analysis we weave into them are grounded in standpoint theory, which draws from material realities of disadvantaged persons to counter entrenched understandings of how the world works—in this case the maternal blame at the heart of young women's[1] relationships with body size and shape. We propose that fat shaming can be inscribed upon the mother's body in ways that become a daughter's inheritance—a practice that is erased when the responsibility and fault for weight gain or loss are offloaded onto mothers. We also hope to present possibilities for and instances of resisting body discipline designed to distance mothers from recovery processes. Our intent is to demonstrate how integral the mother-daughter relationship can be to self and generational healing in contexts that pervasively render female embodiment a problem.

We use a narrative-based approach drawing from a theory notably advanced by Dorothy Smith. She studies the vantage points of people experiencing the material, embodied realities of disadvantage. In particular, she juxtaposes women's experiences against traditional interpretations of women's experiences, for the purpose of disrupting these interpretations. Smith ("Women's Perspective"), along with Mariarosa Dalla Costa and Peggy Morton, propose that social organization can be made sense of from its margins, so these scholars consider gendered labour, such as housework, as their entry-point into larger institutional frameworks. Their research presents the home as a site of work. Home-as-work operates as a critical counterpoint to traditional sociological readings of domestic activities as essentially gendered and private, and not of great significance—not when compared to paid labour of the public sphere. Feminist standpoint scholars have made domestic labour an activity of academic significance by focusing on the personal, day-to-day, and lived experiences of homemaking; they treat cooking, cleaning, childcare, and the like to serious analysis and intimate portrayal.

These frameworks operate along lines of ruling relations, a concept Smith develops to characterize taken-for-granted interactions within a social order. Ruling relations are "forms of consciousness and organization that are objectified" (*Institutional Ethnography*, 13); they are external to consciousness and capable of organizing knowledge along ideological, regulatory lines. Ruling relations are arranged to privilege some and subjugate others through subtle microaggressions that teach people how they ought to behave within the institutions to which they belong. In Smith's example, she describes being chastised for consuming coffee in a hospital ward: "eventually, I could fit this stingy little rule into a whole array of incidents that, tiny in themselves, went together to make up an organization under intense social control" (*Institutional Ethnography as Practice*, 60). This brand of control is "ever present in our lives like the water that fish swim in" (*Institutional Ethnography as Practice*, 105).

We suggest that ruling relations govern a woman's body-work. Our "array of incidents" manifest in and on women's bodies, and enacted through everyday interactions within both maternal relationships and wider social contexts affecting mother and daughter, women old and young. To demonstrate how they operate from the standpoint of women who have internalized and performed and negotiated these rules, we in the following sections take turns presenting reflections on our personal experiences. The narrative work in this chapter entails a shaping of subjectivities and relationships within contexts that devalue and delegitimize through the call to discipline body size and shape.

Samantha: "I'm Sorry I Taught You That"

I cannot remember a time when my mother was not on a diet. And I have worried about my weight for twenty years. Our difficult histories with weight management quietly lurk in the backdrop of the most casual conversations, as when mom and I are sifting through old and new photographs. I always complain about my arms, every single time. Her response lately—captured in the section title "I'm sorry I taught you that"—may well be grounded in her recent grappling with her lived experience as a mother. She has always been critical of her body, and it has lately occurred to her that she has contributed to how critical I have become of mine.

But I do not exist in a cultural vacuum, nor does she. Indeed, she is a product of her culture and my own cultural guide. Debra Gimlin writes the following: "The body is a medium of culture. It is the surface on which prevailing rules of a culture are written. The shared attitudes and practices of social groups are played out at the level of the body, revealing cultural notions of distinctions.... Cultural rules are not only revealed through the body; they also shape the way the body performs and appears" (3). As a medium, an artifact through and upon which cultural rules are enacted and inscribed, the body provides insight into what happens to women's bodies within a patriarchal culture.

This culture dictates that a woman's body is a site of work in constant need of improvement. As Sandra Bartky elaborates, "A woman's face must be made up, that is to say, made over, and so must her body: she is ten pounds 'overweight'; her lips must be made more kissable; her complexion more dewier: her eyes more mysterious" (71). Bartky illustrates here that a woman's body is always a site of work, ever deficient and in need of containment and control.[2] She argues weight gain is connected to a devalued status that must somehow be circumvented. Thinking along with Bartky, I acknowledge my mother is trying to construct herself as something that can be consumed, and, in the process, she is teaching me how to do the same. Naomi Wolf further exposes the cultural framework in which the devaluing of women is cultivated. She unpacks the use of beauty as a way of quantifying and commodifying the value of women by erasing what they may want and by producing in them what heterosexual cismen are conditioned to want: "Each woman has to learn for herself, from nowhere how to feel sexual (though she learns constantly how to look sexual) ... She has very little choice: she must absorb the dominant culture's fantasies as her own" (156). This conflation of women's value with beauty is something women internalize and perform—not simply the impressionable few. The systemic and pervasive nature of everyday microaggressions rendering fat abject is naturalized and taken for granted as true, and is, thus, deeply entrenched and far reaching in scope.

Compounding the problem, mom spent much time advocating for me because I am physically disabled, specifically a wheelchair user with cerebral palsy. She worked at finding ways to make her wheelchair-wielding daughter fit into institutional frameworks not prepared for disability. One such strategy involved ensuring I had thin privilege. It is my thought that she did this out of love, as she was convinced normalization would ensure resources and relationships. If she could not make me walk, she could support me to enact my gender; she could support me to have an aesthetically pleasing and a culturally acceptable body.

I understand my mother as being the impetus for why I am critical of my body, but I question what other recourse she had. She and I experience a culture that does not make space for disabled bodies, and that dictates women are best, worth more, when they are thin. If dominant discourse suggests it is a mother's job to teach weight management, what else was mom to do when navigating my already disadvantaged starting point and advocating for my best interests? How else could she guarantee my success and survival?

Since I have become an academic, a social marker of success, my mother and I have begun to rethink our familial relationship and our collective relationship to weight and body image. She is confident we have matured. I would add the caveat that we now have everything we need, which makes being subversive all the more possible. We are no longer beholden to the level of cultural surveillance exacerbated by poverty. Yet however successfully and ardently we rethink and resist, we cannot escape our culture. Ever bound to ruling relations, mother and I are Smith's fish in the water. Perhaps the subversive response would mean "my arms look fat" becomes a statement only, devoid of a value judgment. Perhaps instead of debating whether my arms are fat and whose fault it is—who is at fault for my body, even who is at fault for my self-critique—we may have more conversations over family photos, while enjoying sugary snacks, about why body aesthetics are so narrow both literally and figuratively. And perhaps one day, if we have the courage to get there, "my arms look fat" will become a celebratory, declarative statement, swelling with body pride.

Jen: Bad Mothers, Difficult Daughters[3]

Often I leafed through those weathered pages faded from sunlight and marked in blue ink, pages featuring their modest desserts, and their happy women, and, most resonant, their charts. The conversion work seemed simple enough to commit to memory, such that mental calculations became my habitus. Food became portion sizes, calorie counts, time commitments for compensatory exercise. Its aesthetics dissolved into numerical equivalents I could tabulate and negotiate throughout the day. My driving purpose was itself numerical: 118, etched into every carton of chocolate milk that taunted me from the refrigerator, every box of cereal in the pantry to discourage quiet frantic moments of binging. That 118 was the bottom threshold of my weight category, so the book of charts claimed.

That book I adopted as canon, that book that first taught me how to watch my weight in concrete and measurable ways was my mother's. Throughout my youth, it would lie about the home, on coffee tables and kitchen counters, whenever she took up the project of weight loss. With the ebb and flow of this tidal routine, she would oftentimes announce her intentions, as though voicing the words made the task real; she would every now and again stock the home with produce and sugar-free snacks, the artifacts of her renewed commitment; she would take me for long walks I remember fondly for the conversations they bore. At minimum, she would herself turn the pages of her instructional booklet, and tell herself that this time the lessons would take hold and produce effect.

It was perhaps because she understood my earnestness around becoming thin[4] that she first encouraged my interest, and it was perhaps because she first encouraged my interest that she blamed herself the night she took me to hospital long after I had left behind, had blown right past, my coveted 118. The years that followed were difficult, my fighting her every suggestion, demand, and plea. I resented when she physically dragged me to a scale, when she contrived I visit a medical professional, and when she took inventory of my caloric consumption. She embodied everything violent about diagnosis and treatment, for as long as I managed to avoid medical care she stood in as my gatekeeper. And she bore my disdain, likely because my survival took priority, perhaps also because she already felt as though she had failed me.

That she might find fault in herself should come as no great surprise, given the ways mothers are implicated in eating disorder diagnoses. But to understand how they are implicated we might first consider the nature of disordered eating itself. The phenomenon has preoccupied feminists since the second wave, whose frame was cultural rather than medical (Chernin *The Obsession*; Orbach; Sontag). To make sense of the condition is to situate it in patriarchal contexts designed to make women feel inferior: "the obsessive and destructive relationship that most women have with their bodies is an internalization of society's relationship to women's bodies—simultaneously one of contempt and worship" (Hutchinson 154). Thinness marks bodies as gendered, and given the ways in which genders are coded, thinness marks bodies as docile: "the cultural fixation on female thinness is ... an obsession about female obedience" (Wolf 97).

Early attempts to characterize eating disorders as cultural did include mothers in their analysis. Kim Chernin (*The Hungry Self*), for example, argues that anorexic behaviours express a daughter's guilt over seeking separation from her mother. The author speaks—nearly hyperbolically—of symbolic matricide, the act of cannibalizing one's mother throughout childhood. Self-starvation is then a reaction to this process of cannibalization, a refusal to continue the practice. To quote Chernin's metaphorical reading of fat or weight gain: "the woman has been taken over by the mother from whom she is trying to separate and whom she has swallowed down, over and over again symbolically in the reenacted primal feast" (*The Hungry Self*, 35).

Such ventures in psychoanalysis, where mothers are symbolically rendered fat and food and called the cause of eating disorders, have impacted treatments, where some behavioural modification strategies are designed to be carried out away from a patient's family, or to change how a patient relates to their mother. The rationale for these recommendations would be that the mother-offspring relationship[5] may produce poor coping strategies, and may have caused the eating disorder in the first place (Beattie; Bruch; Ogden and Steward). Helen Gremillion describes the experiences of patient Maude, who had been diagnosed with anorexia nervosa, and her mother Carol:

> Before Maude's admission, she was seeing a therapist who told Carol not to intervene in Maude's treatment, and staff members at Walsh doubted Carol's ability to be a good mother because she went along with this therapist. But at the same time, the staff expected Carol to hand over to them control of her daughter's health ... no matter how Carol acted in these situations, she could be seen as a "bad mother" (105).

Although I received instruction on weight management through my mother's belongings and behaviours, I no longer seek out ways to cast her in the role of the bad mother. The resentment I once felt for her part in my recovery has since fallen away, and I never truly blamed her for being a conduit. Cultural rules operated within and upon her body, such that she and I shared in struggles with body management. We might have both run calculations through our heads before bringing food to our mouths—driven to the practice because we both experienced rejection and ridicule for fleshy bodies spilling out over ideal dress sizes.

This starting point is important to note, for it served as groundwork for a process of self-healing wherein my mother's refusal to disengage, refusal to leave me entirely at the hands of medical authorities, meant I was spared the more violent instantiations of eating disorder treatment: indefinite incarceration, pharmacological control, and forced feedings. And her quiet shadow work—researching the diagnosis, instructing those around me how to deal with meals, and learning how to meet my needs and understand my patterns—restructured my reality without removing me from my original systems of support. Together, we engaged in collective and collaborative learning over what it means to discipline one's body, and why we expect it of ourselves and encourage it in one another.

Our Stories in Conversation

Demonstrating the application of ruling relations in her interviews with Canadian women who have experienced or undergone weight management, Carla Rice reports the following: "for women with whom

I spoke, early attachments with caretakers represented critical relation-ships where they constructed ideas about gender" (82). She goes on: "mothers actively influenced their embodiment of gender—or participants' incorporation of gender into their psyche and physicality" (82). In some instances, direct instruction was unnecessary, since girls modelled their own femininity by following their mothers' lead: "rather than being told directly that they should fit the standards, some assimilated expectations indirectly through close attunement to their mothers' exertions" (82).

To stop the analysis here may suggest that our mothers would be right to blame themselves for our bad habits or that, more generally, mothers are to blame for passing destructive lessons onto their daughters, even if inadvertently. Yet the substance of what is being transmitted does not itself come from mothers. It comes instead from larger contexts in which patriarchal and fatphobic ideologies are deeply embedded. These ideologies are exchanged and internalized, passed down and through women. As noted, Gimlin (3) considers how cultural rules are inscribed on the body; and Gail Weiss (26) describes the body as a narrative horizon for cultural texts. Particular bodies are produced through culturally expected self-discipline, and thus contain cultural values. Some bodies are marked as failures, others as successes, with standards of measurement found in a system that objectifies and commodifies women's bodies especially.

Rebecca Kukla says the following of the maternal body: "the Unruly Mother, with her dangerously permeable boundaries and her insides capable of creating disorder and monstrosity, has survived and flourished over the last few centuries" (105). This body, she claims, for its softness, its thickness, its messiness, is subjected to social control through reproductive constraint, sexual violence, and, more recently, fat shaming. Speaking specifically of eating disorders, Gremillion characterizes "normalized bodies as the material effects, the corporeal instantiations (over time), of particular sociocultural practices and discourses" (35).

A mother's body may function as a medium through which young girls learn social lessons pertaining to bodily control—that control itself becoming a text, a book to be read. The maternal body specifically, and the feminine body in general, has been culturally framed as transgressive and unruly, and as such, it is subject to monitoring, maintenance, and management. This leaves mothers in a catch-22: they are judged for failing or refusing to engage in self-discipline, as in watching what they eat, or they are at fault should they take up self-discipline and their daughters take notice. Either way, they are framed as the bad mother for not equipping their daughters with the means to succeed in a context where the odds are overwhelmingly and impossibly stacked against them.

It is, therefore, worth applauding even modest attempts at being subversive while conceding how difficult it is to resist the call to discipline female bodies and to resist these lessons being read on our bodies and passed down through our bodies. That shame in relation to weight has a history that can be traced through generations. Mothers and daughters might begin much needed work around redress and resistance by turning to and healing the relations that bring shame to bear on their psyche and physicality, and learning what they might accomplish in solidarity.

Concluding Thoughts

The work we present here is tangled in complicated relations fraught with familial love and sustained feelings of guilt and responsibility. Narrative approaches seeking to portray multiple people, not just the story's subject but the people moving through a subject's life-story, risk co-opting the experiences of others and speculating over their intentions. And given our indebtedness to and appreciation for our own mothers, attempting to illustrate and unpack aspects of our maternal bonds constitutes a sort of betrayal, as we seek to render public some of the intimacies and complications of relationships we have been cultivating since our births—nay, earlier still. But it may well be impossible to tell authentic stories about solitary subjects. As Rosi Braidotti notes, subjectivities are not insular nor isolated, but "based on the immanence of relations" (82), or constellations of relations in process. Our standpoints are entire landscapes of interlocking and intercorporeal relations. We offer a challenge and an alternative to blaming mothers for how women approach body image—not by erasing mothers and their influence from the picture, but by situating maternal relationships in context and by suggesting that there is transformative potential to these relationships.

We might caution here that maternal blame has been culturally possible because caretaking obligations are offloaded onto mothers within patriarchal systems. Although more work needs to be done to trouble expectations that childrearing is entirely or largely a mother's responsibility, we hope this chapter has at least accomplished the feat of resituating mothers in discourses on body management—discourses that have significantly failed in their representations of mothers' roles in the production of abject bodies and appropriate response.

Endnotes

1   In this paper, we are using readings and arguments focusing on impacts on women, and many of these readings take up the term unquestioningly. We are also grounding our analysis in our own social positions, and both authors identify as cisgender women. We recognize, however, that terms like "woman," "mother," and "daughter" imply an insufficiently narrow scope for gender.

2   For the purposes of this chapter, we wish to focus on Bartky's reference to body size. A larger discussion could be had about the culture of makeup use.

3   Our mothers were consulted before this chapter was submitted. My (Jen's) mother in particular would like to contribute that she was honoured by the depiction of her experience and our relationship.

4   It is perhaps more accurate to say I was earnest to become thinner, although this statement—and its qualifier thinner—is contingent on how fatness is interpreted. By the standards set in the diet plan identified in this chapter (and at its heart the body mass index), I was overweight, just flirting with obesity—the next category over. Compared to and in the context of a round working-class family that convened over meals, I was small, just nearly normal, and never discouraged from or shamed over having a second slice of pie or handful of candy. In the schoolyard, I was fat enough for unpopularity and romantic indifference, but not so fat as to draw bullies. I've heard Julie Howe at a conference refer to this state as being "small fats" (2016).

5   While psychoanalytic analysis and strategies have focused on mother-daughter relations, disordered eating is not exclusive to female-identified persons.

Works Cited

Bartky, Sandra. *Femininity and Domination.* Routledge, 1990.

Beattie, Hilary J. "Eating Disorders and the Mother-Daughter Relationship." *International Journal of Eating Disorders*, vol. 7, no. 4, 1988, pp. 453-60.

Braidotti, Rosi. *The Posthuman.* Polity Press, 2013.

Bruch, Hilde. *Eating Disorders: Obesity, Anorexia Nervosa, and the Person Within.* Routledge, 1973.

Chernin, Kim. *The Obsession: Reflections on the Tyranny of Slenderness.* Harper and Row, 1981.

Chernin, Kim. *The Hungry Self: Women, Eating, and Identity.* Random House, 1985.

Dalla Costa, Mariarosa. *The Power of Women and the Subversion of the Community.* Falling Wall Press, 1972.

Gimlin, Debra. *Body Work: Beauty and Self-Image in American Culture.* University of California Press, 2001.

Gremillion, Helen. *Feeding Anorexia: Gender and Power at a Treatment Centre.* Duke University Press, 2003.

Howe, Julie. "Accessing Healthcare in New Zealand as a Fat Woman: 'I am Fat, Therefore I Must be Sick.'" *Fat Studies: Identity, Agency, Embodiment.* Massey University, New Zealand, 2016. Presentation.

Hutchinson, Marcia Germaine. "Imagining Ourselves Whole: A Feminist Approach to Treating Body Image Disorders." *Feminist Perspectives on Eating Disorders*, edited by Patricia Fallon, Melanie Katzman and Susan Wooley, Guilford Press, 1994.

Kukla, Rebecca. *Mass Hysteria: Medicine, Culture, and Mothers' Bodies.*: Rowman and Littlefield Publishers, 2005.

Morton, Peggy. "A Woman's Work is Never Done." *Leviathan*, vol. 2, 1970, pp. 32-47.

Ogden, Jane, and Jo Steward. "The Role of the Mother-Daughter Relationship in Explaining Weight Concern." *International Journal of Eating Disorders*, vol. 28, no. 1, 2000, pp. 78-83.

Orbach, Susie. *Hunger Strike: The Anorectic's Struggle as a Metaphor for Our Age.* Norton, 1979.

Rice, Carla. *Becoming Women: The Embodied Self in Image Culture.* Toronto: University of Toronto Press, 2014. Print.

Smith, Dorothy E. "Women's Perspective as a Radical Critique of Sociology." *Sociological Inquiry*, vol. 44, no. 1, 1974, pp. 7-33.

Smith, Dorothy E. *Institutional Ethnography: A Sociology for People.* AltaMira Press, 2005.

Smith, D.E.. *Institutional Ethnography as Practice.* Rowman & Littlefield Publishers, Inc., 2006.

Sontag, Susan. *Illness as Metaphor.* Penguin, 1983.

Weiss, Gail. "The Body as a Narrative Horizon." *Thinking the Limits of the Body,* edited by Jeffrey Jerome Cohen and Gail Weiss, State University of New York Press, 2003, pp. 25-38.

Wolf, Naomi. *The Beauty Myth.* Vintage Canada, 1991.

Untitled R.A.

Chapter Seven

Esau: Curse, Stare, Courage

Natasha Galarraga

Curse

"You are going to get the curse soon!" my grandmother, slightly intoxicated, wailed over the patio table. I always detested family gatherings, especially when I was a preteen. On this occasion, to my utter embarrassment, I was being questioned about the status of my period. Fat for my age and being on the verge of changing into a woman, the extra eyes glaring at my body always hurt my stomach and turned my face the brightest shade of red. The aunts came over to where I was seated, and all three of them started poking at my breasts. Mockingly they hissed, "They are getting bigger!" Hearty wine-fuelled belly laughs followed. My grandmother, mother, and aunts are all very well endowed. I suspect they were checking to see if I would keep up the family tradition.

My grandmother was the self-proclaimed great beauty of the family. I didn't know her in her prime, but when intoxicated, she spoke of it often. I knew the soft, short, round, grandmother. I knew the strong and determined grandmother who commanded a brood of nine for the most part single handed. But when intoxicated, she would hold court at these gatherings and speak of her small waist, thick, luminous chocolate brown hair, and many admirers.

My aunt's property in Oakville, where we had all the family gatherings during the summers of my youth, was large with many flower gardens. I inevitably always needed to walk to the furthest garden in order to be alone and breathe again. This garden had a clawed foot tub that daises sprung out of like smiling companions. They would sway in the breeze, waving me over. I always knelt beside the tub, intertwined my chubby fingers, and started praying. I prayed at this occasion repeatedly to never get my period, to never have the curse. The daisies smiled at me, and I smiled back. Strangely, in that moment I knew I would never be cursed. I would never be like them.

Stare

When I was nineteen, I remember looking at myself naked in a full-length mirror and being truly horrified at what reflected back at me. I had avoided the full-length bathroom mirror for a long time, placing an old sheet over it that covered more than half of the mirror. I was nearing three hundred pounds, with more hair than usual covering my body for a girl my age. I was experiencing very irregular periods, which was oddly never cause for worry, since I was still a virgin. Dark patches of thicker textured skin also started developing between my thighs, underarms, and around my neck. Large clumps of hair would tumble into the shower drain when I washed my long mane, and a slight widow's peak was forming along my hairline.

Hair grew first thick on my sideburns and upper lip eventually coming in like two landing strips on the underside of my chin. Every night, I would spend countless hours with my face in an old seventies' makeup mirror, plucking hairs from my chin. The acid green tinted light that the mirror emitted was the best for plucking the short dark hairs.

I learned the various painful methods of hair removal from an early age. I soon perfected the arts of shaving, plucking, waxing, and bleaching. Different parts of my body required different treatments at different times of the day or week. The fingers, toes, and around the nipples would get hair bleach, since the hair was much finer in those areas. The appendages, navel area, and vulva would require shaving or waxing, and the chin and eyebrows always required regular tweezing. Hair removal became an integral part of my daily routine. These hair removal rituals were time consuming and gruelling but necessary. However, these rituals bred resentment and bitterness in me as they were performed. A darkness swelled inside of me, fuelled by these emotions. Unlike the hair, it was not so easy to remove.

On the day I was forced to take stock of my full appearance, I had let the hair on my body grow out for about a month. I had finished high school early and had from January to September off before starting university. I ceased all grooming rituals. Not purposefully– I were shunning these practices that helped me fit in a bit better in high school, or, at least stand out a bit less – but in a passive way, like somewhere deep in my brain I had concluded that there was no need to engage in these time-consuming and seemingly endless hair-removal activities.

It was winter, and the basement bathroom where the infamous mirror hung was cold. Too cold to fog up. The sheet had fallen off the mirror during my shower, and when I pulled back the shower curtain, I gasped. My skin tone, which is fair, from a slight distance looked darker, since my legs and arms were covered in a thick, dark mass of wet hair. Hair ran up from the pubic area encircling my navel. Light fuzzy patches grew around my nipples, and when I turned around, I could see dark fuzz in the small of my back. I stared at myself for a long time that day; the hair on my head fell limp around my round face. Worst of all, I could see a dark shadow on the underside of my chin growing, the forming of a beard. Bizarrely, at this moment, I remembered clearly the prayers at my aunt's bathtub garden. I stared and stared at myself in the mirror. I had cursed myself.

Courage

My mother's cooking is glorious—her dishes are often full of cream, butter, sugar, salt, the best olive oil, and succulent cuts of meat. Every dinner ended with homemade dessert, and there were always seconds. She is large women herself, but this was always glossed over by the fact that she had three children, two of which are twins. In her opinion, there was no reason for me to be heavy. She just felt I ate too much, as she would tell me while she ladled more creamy mashed potatoes on to my plate.

I was in high school at the beginning of the Internet craze. We didn't have a home computer yet, so information about weight loss was limited to old *Weight Watchers* magazines of my grandmother's, TV, or second-hand knowledge from friends at school. My mother is very territorial about the kitchen. Pointing to recipes from a 1980s *Weight Watchers* magazine just irritated her. She would quickly retaliate by pointing out the fact that my sisters and my father were not fat from her cooking. When I suggested purchasing exercise equipment or getting a gym membership, she suggested I do more chores around the house.

My parents glared at me constantly during this time with a mixture of disgust and fear. They never mentioned the growing hair on my face but commented consistently on my weight. I think the former was too much to process emotionally for both of them. It was easier to ignore that issue. Sadly, they left me to traverse the world of rare illnesses all alone, but worst of all, they left me with the very firm belief I had brought this all on myself.

The medical community was no kinder to deal with. In one of my more memorable conversations with my family doctor, he repeatedly told me that my symptoms were due to being "obese." He stressed the importance of preventing weight gain, in particular "abdominal obesity," as he eyed my robust belly with contempt. A very young and scared me left his office feeling completely defeated. After that, I stopped going to all doctors for a long time. I suffered with the symptoms silently, and held to my daily rituals like a life raft.

A number of small indignities rallied me to find the courage to finally seek out answers. The rituals that I was clinging to for peace of mind were slowly starting to disintegrate. The thick layers of foundation I needed to put on my face before leaving the house every day to hide my facial stubble needed constant reapplying. I probably drew more attention to my face this way rather than hiding the problem. Then there was the time I went to a party, during which a very intoxicated boy grabbed me from behind, placing his hands under my shirt. He ran his hands up my lower back, paused, looked at me crossed eyed and said drunkenly, "Do you shave your back?" These mortifications were painful and, unfortunately, growing in number. I started searching a very content deficient nineties' Internet and began reading books at the public library about bearded ladies of the sideshow. From my very rudimentary research, I pieced together a possible cause for these symptoms. I deduced the solution seemed to reside with a gynecologist. Shortly after learning this, I acquired an appointment.

Life can burn so hot sometimes, especially when faced with the truth. My face was tingling, with sweat collecting under my eyes and above my lip, as I sat in the gynecologist's office. A doctor was actually acknowledging everything that I had suspected about myself for so many years, and my body was reacting to this confirmation with a mixture of panic and relief. The gynecologist had an understanding tone to his voice. He asked if I had the following long list of symptoms: irregular periods, excess facial and body hair (hirsutism), adult acne or severe adolescent acne, male-pattern baldness, weight gain, skin tags, general overall thinning hair, increased blood sugar, or darkening and thickening of the skin on the neck, groin, underarms, or skin folds. I nodded my head to the symptoms I had, and he kept stopping to ask if he should continue. I had to reassure him that I was fine at several points in that conversation and urged him to resume. He continued by listing the grim long-term health consequences of a disease called polycystic ovarian syndrome (PCOS), and said all symptoms can worsen with obesity, but it can be difficult for girls and women with PCOS to lose weight. The doctor quickly scrawled down on his prescription pad the name of the birth control pill that would help manage some of the symptoms. The moment he handed it to me, it started to dissolve in my sweaty hands. He then spoke very gently, "Everything will be better from now on." I shook his hand firmly with my damp palm and felt relieved for the first time since the curse arrived in my life.

Epilogue

Polycystic ovarian syndrome (PCOS) is a lifelong disorder with different clinical manifestations across one's lifespan. The road has been bumpy since my initial diagnosis, and has been filled with countless laser appointments, extreme diets, depression, and social anxiety. Laser in the early days was painful. I often had to sit with an icepack on my face for an hour after a treatment to let the swelling go down, for only moderate results in hair reduction.

I have binged on every greasy, sweet, and carb-infused food creation, and I have spent countless hours in the gym to contrast my many months on the couch. I have had moments of scrutinizing every tidbit of food entering my body, and I have felt triumphant on days that I starved myself. On those days, I felt powerful and in control—"this is what thin people must feel like!" Unfortunately, I only ever felt that way due to unhealthy experimenting with whatever diet pills I could get my doctor to prescribe for me. When the pills eventually were taken off the market (as they always would be), all the weight would return. My triumph was always fleeting, and letting numbers on a scale determine your self-worth is a dangerous mind game to play.

Despite all the hurt, life can also be miraculous. Slowly over time, I found others like myself in appearance and temperament. Their kindness and understanding helped me to start to gradually let go of the self-hate, self-doubt, and shame that dominated my youth. Also, conversing with others struggling with this disease has aided in dispelling the darkness I carried around inside myself for so long. By punching my darkness into the sunlight, I finally accepted myself with warmth and love.

Chapter Eight

Dear Mom

Sam Abel

I both resent it and understand what you are trying to do.
We are so strained that perhaps making food is the only way for you to show me that you care.

When I try to decline, you don't listen.

You won't take no for an answer.

But all you say to yourself is no. You can't feed yourself like you feed everyone else.

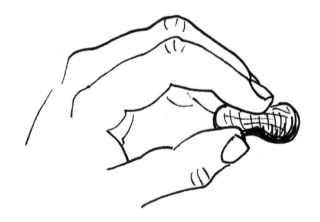

You love peanuts.
But the peanut is not just a snack,
it's a minefield.

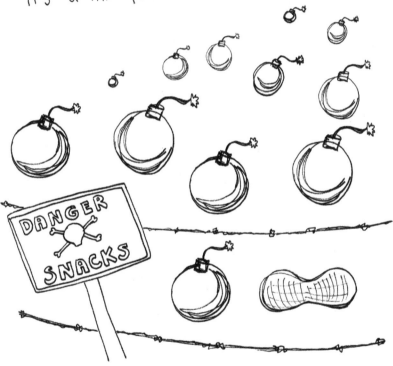

A failure that you need to explain away, to apologize for.

You are not bad, Mom. You are hungry.

When I am hungry, I apologize for nothing.

And it confuses you.

Despite being stuck with a fat kid, you never put me on a diet.

But I've watched you diet, count calories,
go on exercise binges. You remind yourself of
how thin you were before you had me.

No matter how many conversations we have about my politics.

I can't get you to turn off the weightloss shows.

Or put down the "health" magazines

You are hyperfocused on your body's "failings" and you always, inspite of our conversations about fat acceptance, tell me that I've lost weight when you are trying to give me a compliment.

Instead of feeding me, why don't you listen to me?

And when you are hungry, why don't you listen to yourself?

The older we get, the more poorly we communicate, and the more fixated you get on feeding me.

A solution that doesn't fix problems that we can't name.

I'm sorry.

Happiness Projects and Close Bonds: A Calorie-Counting Mother and Her Fat, Feminist Killjoy Daughter

Crystal Kotow

In 2007, I embarked on what would become the first and last major weight-loss period of my life. Two phenomena influenced my desire to lose weight: first, my doctor had put me on hormonal birth control and I was concerned about its connection to blood clots, and second, my mother was experiencing astonishing success losing weight using a calorie-counting program, a no frills version of Weight Watchers based solely on counting calories instead of points. I wanted to feel as good about myself as my mother seemingly did. For six months, I ate no more than twelve hundred calories per day and engaged in vigorous cardio exercise five out of seven days per week. I lost approximately one hundred pounds very quickly, but after six months, my body gave up on me. Initially energized, I was eventually tired and cold all of the time. I was self-conscious to a degree I had never experienced, and I was hungry—I was very, very hungry.

As it does for the majority of people who undergo major weight loss, the weight started coming back (Bacon and Aphramor 1). It did not matter how little I ate or how much I exercised, my body rebelled against me, its abuser. I recognize now that it was my body simply trying to keep me alive, but I resented myself then. My mother's weight loss was ongoing and I was failing.

Two years later, several pounds fatter, I was still struggling with my growing body as I conducted research for the literature review of my master's project. Exploring representation of fat bodies on television led me to corners of the Internet I never knew existed. For instance, I found the online fat acceptance community and was immediately bewildered, yet empowered, by the idea that I could be fat and free from dieting. Thus, began a very different type of weight-related journey. Since 2009, I have considered myself part of the fat acceptance movement—a movement of fat activists that rejects violent messages about the worthlessness of fat bodies and about weight loss at any cost as the path to health. Fat activists support fostering an accepting and loving relationship with the body as it is now.

My experience as a reformed dieter, my mother's journey as a continued dieter, and my academic interest in affect theory—specifically Sara Ahmed's work around happiness—leave me with various questions about thinness as happiness. I was under the impression that once I had lost enough weight, I would be happy. As far as I could tell, the only thing between me and my happiness was extra weight, and if I worked hard enough, spent money on the right food and gym memberships, and fought against all of the cues my body sent me that it was suffering, then I could access real happiness. At the same time, my mother, who, at the time of this writing, is thinner than I have ever known her to be, seems to be very content with her body and the way she maintains it— even though it involves attending weekly weigh-ins and meetings where women punish themselves if they have gained weight by announcing it to their group and then enduring the public shaming.

In this chapter, I explore how fat politics and dieting affect the relationship between my mother and me. Using Ahmed's work on happiness, I theorize weight loss and thinness as "happy objects," illuminate my role as an "affect alien," and work through the complex nature of maintaining a deeply loving and caring relationship between me—a woman who is anti-intentional weight loss and holds radical fat body politics—and my mother, a woman who continues to believe in the happiness promised by achieving a thinner body.

Thinness as a Happy Object

In her work *Happy Objects*, Ahmed defines objects of happiness as not only physical or material things, "but also anything that we imagine might lead us to happiness, including objects in the sense of values, practices, and styles, as well as aspirations ... The promise of happiness takes this form: that if you have this or that or do this or that, then happiness is what follows" (41). North American attitudes toward fatness frame fat bodies as grotesque, lazy, incapable, lacking hygiene, undesirable, and unlovable (Erdman Farrell 34). By default, the notion that one can be fat and happy is rejected by mass society, an idea aided by a diet and beauty industry that fosters and maintains insecurities around body size and appearance in general. These industries present solutions to the body problems they create, and I suggest, using Ahmed's definition of happy objects, that these solutions themselves are happy objects—they hold the promise of thinness, and in a culture that demonizes fatness, thinness itself promises happiness.

Curiously, at my thinnest, I was the least happy I had ever felt. I had bought into, literally and figuratively, the idea that a smaller body would make me feel better overall; instead, my self-esteem and quality of life plummeted. Ahmed claims happiness involves a particular type of intentionality that she describes as "end oriented." Meaning, that oftentimes it is not simply that we are made happy by something as it exists in the present but that certain things "become happy *for us*, if we imagine they will bring happiness *to us*" (emphasis in original, "Happy Objects" 33). She describes happiness as something that we aim for—a goal, an endpoint—as opposed to the means to that end.

So-called solutions to fatness are themselves happy objects because of how they are imbued with the promise of happiness; these solutions are a means to an end and happy objects. But using the conceptualization of happiness as an end goal—and keeping in mind that thinness itself promises happiness—my feelings of happiness should have steadily increased as my body became thinner. Where is the disconnect? Ahmed explains that our expectations of happy objects are shaped in particular ways and that even if something fails to live up to our expectations, we still "arrive at objects with an expectation of how we will be affected by them" ("Happy Objects" 41). How I felt in my smaller body did not meet my expectations. And I think we can theorize this disconnect through its connection to power. Power—mass media, diet and beauty industries—maintains the idea that thinness promises happiness, so even when countless people experience little to no happiness from a supposed happy object (in this case, thinness), that object retains its status as a happy object. This may explain rates of yo-yo dieting. Despite hard evidence that diets do not work and attempts at weight loss are futile, the diet industry continues to thrive and solutions to weight problems continue to sell. The diet industry promises happiness, but it relies on violent attitudes and actions toward the eradication of fat bodies. My fat body politics are based primarily on this premise.

The Fat Feminist Killjoy

My body politics put me at odds with many people, and I have learned to embrace this because my politics are rooted in social justice. This concern for justice ensures I take advantage of opportunities to interrupt and to question harmful actions and speech acts. Consistently being the person who interjects when discussions turn racist, homophobic, sexist, ableist, transphobic, fatphobic, and so on, is exhausting. Ahmed introduces two figures that capture this experience: affect aliens and feminist killjoys.

One becomes an affect alien when they "do not experience pleasure from proximity to objects that are already attributed as being good" ("Happy Objects" 37). Ahmed explains that when we do not feel pleasure from objects deemed good, we may doubt ourselves and wonder if there's something wrong with us. She also writes that the disappointment experienced when happy objects do not make us feel the way we expected can result in rage toward whoever or whatever promised that happiness in the first place ("Happy Objects" 37).

Regarding my own shift from being diet minded to rejecting the diet mentality, my feelings of sadness and low self-esteem in my smaller body did alienate me from those around me who were losing weight and seemingly loving life (at that point, it was more than just my mother wrapped up in her weight-loss journey). The shift was gradual. I spent years loathing my body for steadily gaining weight, despite my newfound liberating body politics. This was a time of confusion. On one hand, I was alienated from people invested in the idea of happiness promised by thinness because I wholly rejected actively pursuing weight loss in any form; and on the other hand, I felt alienation from fat acceptance because I knew that I still wanted my body to maintain its smaller size, and I experienced frustration with continuous weight gain that levelled out five years after the significant weight loss.

During this period of confusion, my feminist and body politics intensified. Not only did I find myself actively derailing uncritical conversations about weight loss, I also became more comfortable, in general, confronting people who expressed problematic opinions and ideas. This marked the birth of my identification with Ahmed's "feminist killjoy":

> Feminists might kill joy simply by not finding the objects that promise happiness to be quite so promising. The word *feminism* is thus saturated with unhappiness. Feminists by declaring themselves as feminists are already read as destroying something that is thought of by others not only as being good but as the cause of happiness. The feminist killjoy "spoils" the happiness of others; she is a spoilsport because she refuses to convene, to assemble, or to meet up over happiness ("The Promise of Happiness" 65)

My identification with the feminist killjoy was so strong I eventually branded myself "fat feminist killjoy." Intentionally adding the word "fat" ensures there is no mistaking my willingness to make trouble in the face of body shaming specifically. My fat body makes trouble—is troubling for many—by simply existing. Supplementing my corporeal reality with my voice, being outspoken about the violence of fatphobia, further serves to illuminate the disconnect between dieting, weight loss, and happiness.

Affect aliens do not experience happiness from objects that promise it. Feminist killjoys kill the happiness people experience from problematic happy objects. What is the relationship between the two? Can they exist independent of each other? I suppose one must experience alienation from happy objects before they can decide to speak out against the joy others experience from these objects. This is to say that before a person can recognize and fight injustice, they must be awakened to it in some form or another. The feminist killjoy cannot exist without the affect alien. I suggest, however, that the affect alien can exist without the feminist killjoy because a person can experience negative affects without deciding to fight injustice by killing joy when opportunities present themselves.

Happy Objects: Family Bonds versus Diet Culture

In *The Promise of Happiness*, Ahmed refers to the family as a happy object. We are supposed to be made happy by familial bonds. She also identifies family as a unit through which we can explore different ideas of happiness without destroying bonds when these ideas come into conflict (46-47). I have established that my body politics do not align with my mother's. I am anti-intentional weight loss, and she is a proud member of Calorie Counters. I champion taking up space as she continues to shrink. For me, food is emotional, enjoyable, social, whereas for my mother, food is still moralized (good versus bad), and associated with numbers and math (calories). At a higher level, however, my mother and I have an unbreakable bond. I consider her my best friend, and I am her biggest fan. She has cared for me in ways only she knows how for thirty-two years, and I can count on her to continue to do so. As I age, I find myself invested in caring for her, too. Part of that care involves my knowing how good it feels to divest myself from the mental and emotional violence inflicted by diet culture, and wanting her to feel just as liberated.

We have had to learn to exist together, to know each other, to care for each other, despite our differing body politics because the mother-daughter bond—our relationship—matters most. But what does this maintenance ask of us?

As it happens, my mother's relationship with her mother was difficult. My grandmother was a tall, strong, and lean woman. She prided herself on appearances and did not respect variation in body size, in women especially. My mother was relatively lean until she had children, but on various occasions, she recounted me with tales of my grandmother making comments about my mother's weight when she was a child. This is, of course, one way we learn to feel shame for our bodies. Grandma never approved of my mother's fatness, and certainly did not appreciate my sister and me for our fatness. Shame was abundant. My grandmother's forms of encouragement to lose weight manifested as offers to fund gym memberships and reminders that if I wanted my crush to like me back, "you know what you have to do."

I choose to share this brief look at the legacy of body hate in my family to set a stage for discussion of what liberation looks like to my mother and me. Mom began her weight loss journey in 2006; she lost enough weight very quickly to garner attention from everyone who knew her. She relished her newfound body and the confidence that came as a result of the attention. In that moment, I was both proud and jealous of her. As I mentioned previously, her weight loss success was part of what inspired my own attempt.

She made the decision to pursue weight loss after feeling something inside her crack when she bent down one day. She also knew she was not getting any younger and that if her body felt sore now, it was not going to get better without intervention. Intervention is used intentionally here; there were various ways she could have intervened in her body's journey through age, but weight loss was her choice. I wonder if in a culture that promotes weight loss as the only reasonable path to health, there is even any choice at all.

For about a year, I attended Calorie Counters meetings with her. At this point, I was gaining back weight I had lost during my time starving myself and exercising excessively. Each meeting I reported weight gain; I felt such self-loathing as the group said in unison "we're glad you're here." The meetings were ritualistic: arrive, weigh-in, sit in a circle, share your weight gain or loss for the week, and listen to someone lecture on any number of topics related to weight loss. No one ate supper before attending the meeting out of fear it would throw off their weigh-in. For me, it was never more than people gathered weekly in a room to build community around hatred for their bodies.

These meetings were supposed to help the women in attendance reach happiness: thinner bodies are happy objects. And for my mother, the struggle to lose weight was of no consequence once she started to receive positive feedback on and from her body. She had seemingly acquired her happy object while mine continued to grow further from me.

When I graduated from my master's and was better equipped with a critical lens through which to view diet and weight-loss culture, it was easy for my mother and me to have blow-out fights over body politics. For her, fatness was the enemy. For me, hating my body into something others would approve of was the enemy. For my mother, liberation was connected to a more mobile body, a slimmer body, a body that fit into fashionable clothing, a sense of control over the body, and attention received by her shrinking body. For me, liberation was and is connected to being mentally and emotionally free from viewing body size as imbued with value, from seeing food through a moralistic lens, and from striving to shrink a body that will not be tamed.

Ahmed writes about the crisis experienced by the feminist killjoy. She explains that in a world where there is so much to be against, anger "can spill at those who happen to be nearby, who are the closest to us." She continues:

> How easily in being against something we can risk those who are with us, who are for us, who we are with and for; we can risk them because they are before us. Our anger when generalized against the injustice of the world, can become directed toward those who happen to be nearest, which is often those who are dearest ... sometimes even when the consequences of saying something are regrettable we cannot regret saying something, because not saying something would have been even more regrettable. ("A Killjoy in Crisis" para.18)

Of course, my mother is my nearest and my dearest. And at that time, staying silent on issues of body politics would have harmed my mental health more than our disagreements harmed our relationship. At one point, my mother decided it was not worth fighting with me over these differing politics. Since neither of us was going to change our minds, conversations about weight loss and dieting died out. Repairing the damage associated with feeling as if my mother disproved of my body took time.

The affective labour we both employed to keep our relationship intact involved active acceptance of principles of bodily autonomy. Although I might not have approved of the means by which she sought her liberation, I learned to respect her freedom to do with her body what she felt was right. In addition to this acceptance, I found myself wanting to know her again. My politics strengthened while I was still young and stubborn. Deviation from what I felt was right meant others were wrong, and it was my job to intervene. I killed joy, to be sure, but failed to hold space for differing subjectivities.

I learned that to care for my mother in a more productive way, I needed to listen to her. I learned that no issue is black and white and that her smaller body did not mean she saw no value in my choice to no longer try to shrink mine. I learned to value complexity and complicatedness. I no longer sought to kill her joy because as far as I could (and still can) see, she was not (is not) unhappy.

What is at stake when radical and progressive personal politics threaten family relationships, effectively "killing joy" and sabotaging someone else's happiness project? The stakes were too high for me in this case. Losing the relationship with my mother was a very real potential consequence had I pushed my politics even further. Pulling back felt wrong at first and in many ways weak, as if I were betraying the fat acceptance movement—a movement that had given me back my life. But pulling back also opened up space for growth, both personally and interpersonally. We work to understand each other. We continue to love each other.

Endnote

1   Recognizing the privilege of my position as a white, able-bodied, middle-class, cis woman is important. For instance, my mother would never have kicked me out of her home or physically harmed me for disagreeing with intentional weight loss. My life was not at risk as a result of identifying as a feminist killjoy. My relationship to my body does not carry legacies of racism, ableism, classism, or heterosexism. Discrimination based on body size is well documented (Puhl and Brownell), but it's a fact that I do not have to manage the majority of intersections of body size with other axes of oppression, which shapes the outcomes of my experiences in particular, often less dangerous, ways.

Works Cited

Ahmed, Sara. "Happy Objects." *The Affect Theory Reader*, edited by Melissa Gregg and Gregory J. Seigworth. Duke University Press, 2010, pp. 29-51.

Ahmed, Sara. *The Promise of Happiness*. Duke University Press, 2010.

Ahmed, Sara. "A Killjoy in Crisis." *Feminist Killjoys*. 28 Aug. 2014, feministkilljoys.com/2014/08/28/a-killjoy-in-crisis/. Accessed 12 Aug. 2018.

Bacon, Linda, and Lucy Aphramor. "Weight Science: Evaluating the Evidence for a Paradigm Shift." *Nutrition Journal*, vol. 10, no. 9, 2011, pp. 1-13.

Erdman Farrell, Amy. *Fat Shame: Stigma and the Fat Body in American Culture.* New York University Press, 2011.

Puhl, Rebecca, and Kelly Brownell. "Bias, Discrimination, and Obesity." *Obesity*, vol. 9, no. 12, 2001, pp. 788-805.

Puhl, Rebecca, and Kelly Brownell. "Confronting and Coping with Weight Stigma: An Investigation of 'Overweight' and Obese Adults." *Obesity*, vol. 14, no. 10, 2006, pp. 1802-15.

Section III:
Coming to Term(s):
Fat Motherhood

Sky Woman, Mother Emma Day

Chapter Ten

From Famine to Feast: Pregnancy and Motherhood

Liz Nelson

I was fat before I got pregnant, and I was fat after I was pregnant. What happened during that pregnancy was completely unexpected—I lost weight.

It makes me think about the moments in my life when I have dramatically lost weight. Sure, there is that expansion in the thighs and contraction in the waist that happens whenever I get caught up in some athletic pursuit for a few months, and I definitely go through a gentle waxing and waning over the course of a day, a week, a year. There's also the gradual fat escalator that has followed me through adolescence, high school, university, and the workplace—my body expanding and aging in perfect step. But those big, dramatic weight losses were associated with periods of intense stress and sadness—the eviscerating loss of my mother, the discovery of an infidelity, an unplanned and unwanted move.

But I lost weight while pregnant. Yes, it's a stressful time. But it was also a time for celebration—this was something that my partner and I had created through painstaking emotional labour—the agonizing selection of a sperm donor, the painful navigation of the fertility industry, the personal questions from complete strangers who just *need* to know how two women can make a baby. That pregnancy was a triumph! But then why was I wasting away, losing pieces of myself as she grew inside of me?

The morning sickness was certainly the primary culprit, lasting all the way into my seventh month, which coincided with a diagnosis of gestational diabetes. Even as I was regaining interest in food, I was forced to closely monitor everything I was eating, strictly limiting some of my favourite things. And of course, there was the loss of one of my favourite foods for all nine months—the sweet tang of a cheap shiraz, the icy feel of a can of a beer against my lips. All these things contributed.

I had been ready to grow. I had been excited to experience an increase in size that was societally accepted and rewarded. All the shame about fertility and fatness was behind me, and I looked damn fine in those flowy maternity dresses. But I was losing a relationship at the same time—one that I had taken for granted for such a long time but that was deeply fulfilling and formed dense scaffolding protecting so many different parts of my life. And that breakup was with food.

Food and I became enemies. I resented food. I hated having to eat it, day after day, disgusted by its presence in my life. Choosing what to eat from an array of unappetizing options, experiencing an uptick in nausea every time I waited too long. Months of estrangement from something that used to bring me such joy, used to add colour to every corner of my life.

In the days following our daughter's birth, I ate everything. In those voracious months of nursing, I took pleasure in the crushed banana bread at the bottom of the diaper bag, I relished every opportunity to have seconds, and then thirds. I regained the weight. I gained a little more. I hit my lifetime maximum and surpassed it. I ate and I celebrated, I ate and I reclaimed myself.

I am fatter than I was. There is more of me. And my love of food and drink and feeling just a bit too full is back.

And I still look fabulous in those flowy maternity dresses. In fact, they might just fit better on me now.

Sharing Emma Day

Chapter Eleven

Crazy, Squishy Love: How I Learned to Love My Body through the Eyes of My Son

Jodi Christie

"Mama, why is your belly so squishy?" These were the first words out of my three-year-old's mouth one morning. We still co-sleep, and we were in that precious moment where we were both awake but not ready to extricate ourselves from the warm bed, particularly in the depths of winter. Typically, these fleeting moments are reserved for cuddling, talking in hushed tones about what our plans may be for the day, rolling from side to side under the covers and revelling in the extra time weekends afford. We have a chance to gradually dip our toes into the real world, full of obligations and schedules, instead of hurling ourselves into it like we normally do on weekdays. On these rare occasions, there is no particular rush. We're just meant to enjoy each other.

His comment interrupted my thought process. Everything came to a grinding halt in my mind. My belly was squishy. I had just heard it from the most reliable source.

I told him that my belly had grown when he was inside of it. I told him that it's a miracle, really, that a mother's skin can stretch to accommodate a growing human being inside of her own body.

"What was your belly like before I was in it?" he asked.

"Pretty much the same," I lied in an attempt to avoid any feeling of culpability on his part. Neither he nor I was prepared to talk about the complexities of how a body changes when a child has made it their home for nine months—how they kick and stretch and transform a portion of your physical self into their own temporary lodging. That occupied space doesn't just go away after they're forcefully evicted from your cozy womb. Your internal organs shift. Everything changes.

To provide some context to all of this, I need to go back to when I was a teenager. My sister, who was my best friend growing up (and still is to this very day), began struggling with an eating disorder at the age of twelve. I subsequently developed my own pattern of disordered eating. I hesitate to say that it was partially because of my sister's food restrictions, but I can't help but feel as if I were constantly trying to mirror her behaviour. She was my idol.

Eventually, we were both hospitalized due to extreme and unhealthy weight loss, and they did lots of tests on us because we were a sibling pair with eating disorders. We were quite rare, though not in a valuable way like a jewel, but it was a perfect opportunity for the doctors to investigate the possibility of a genetic basis for the disease. Neither of us minded being poked and prodded with needles. We had given up on most things. And if they didn't administer a feeding tube, we considered that a good day. My sister moved away for school in 1998, and I was devastated. I didn't know who I was without her. But I finished up my final year at high school and moved on to another city the following year.

In university and throughout my early twenties, I was well known for being the person who was constantly exercising and heavily restricting what I ate. One of my first jobs in Toronto, my new city, was at a restaurant, and I was constantly being offered food. It became somewhat of a running joke that I would turn nearly everything down, and one of my best friends took it upon herself to be my unofficial spokesperson. So when someone would offer me a piece of cake or a plate of fries, she would swoop in and block their advance with what soon became a catchphrase of sorts: "She can't eat that." Although it sounds lighthearted and more like an inside joke rather than a dangerous pattern of eating, I was in a great deal of emotional pain. I used to love these green gummy frogs, and they were one of the only sweets I ever allowed myself to have. After weighing myself at the gym one day and discovering I had gained three ounces, I cut those out entirely, too.

Constantly being vigilant and endlessly patrolling what enters your body is time consuming, and it's also exhausting trying to explain it to people who notice these behaviours. Or rather, it's exhausting trying to come up with excuses. I started to supplement food with recreational drug use, which was probably my answer, on some level, to constantly restricting other areas in my life. Thankfully, this period didn't last long. Being self-medicated, undernourished, and sleep deprived is truly not a path that sets you up for much future success.

In 2004, my sister had moved back from Victoria, and the two of us got an apartment together in Toronto. It was so wonderful to be back together with her again but, somewhat predictably, two people with such disordered eating habits were probably not the best match in terms of roommates. We fed off each other; we normalized the behaviour for each other. We lasted a year before we went our separate ways.

As I moved into my professional career, I migrated through different groups of friends and didn't always feel like explaining why I wouldn't have a piece of cake for someone's birthday at an office party. I avoided social situations involving food. And social situations involving food are pretty much all of them, if you think about it. I had successfully isolated myself and, as a result, grappled daily with feelings of loneliness. I remember at one of my first days at a new job, the receptionist, Michelle, became so annoyed with me when I refused the cookies on offer in the breakroom that she took it upon herself to make my life miserable whenever there happened to be food lying about. And, most days, there would be pastries in the morning, leftover pizza at lunch from a client meeting, or afternoon snacks, so it felt like navigating a minefield.

To add to the list of ways in which I was punishing and policing myself, I started exercising compulsively. I would push myself to the point of being physically ill. I recall that after one particular workout in January 2007, I was making my way home and had to sit down in a snowbank because I was dizzy and disoriented. The combination of intense physical activity and heavily restricted caloric intake had made me feel like my head was swimming. I don't recall how long I sat there. I don't even remember if I had been conscious the entire time.

There was also a brief period in which I was abusing diuretics. They made me feel confused and aggressive, and my heart would speed up so much sometimes that it would frighten me, so I stopped. Things could have gone horribly wrong, but I wasn't considering the risks. I wanted the results. Somehow amid all of that chaos, I felt in control of my body and its capabilities.

In actuality, I was flailing.

My sister was hospitalized at Toronto General Hospital several years after we had moved out of our shared apartment. The first time that I visited her I walked into the eating disorder ward and saw her sitting there, alone and frail. Her skin looked grey, and she seemed so small and hunched over. She was knitting quietly and didn't see me watching her. I cried. And when she turned and saw me standing there, she cried too. We held each other for a really long time.

When I found out that I was pregnant, which was a surprise for me, I immediately had to let go of the body I knew. I found myself doing that without an ounce of resentment. I was so happy. I smothered my giant belly in cocoa butter and marvelled at my silhouette in the mirror. The glistening skin was a shining testament to its function. It was making room for a small person to grow. I was overwhelmed by how beautiful the process felt. I never once considered how it would affect my body in the long term. That seemed so far away and irrelevant.

Four years later, I wouldn't trade my son for the flattest belly in the world. I consider my squishiness a daily reminder of my crazy, uncontrollable mom love for him. I did tell him that it's never a good idea to comment on someone's body or physical appearance. I reinforce that a person's appearance is only a very small representation of who they actually are in this world.

Ultimately, would I wish for a nonsquishy belly? Maybe. But then, would he miss resting his head on its softness? I think I'll stay exactly the way I am, just in case.

Feeding Emma Day

Chapter Twelve

Mother to Daughter: From Fat Hatred to Fat Love in One Hundred Years

Jennifer Lee

Nanna

When my grandmother was a child, she ate the warm wax from the candle burning in her room at night in an attempt to fill her empty belly. She grew up during the Depression in rural Tasmania, Australia, and sucked pebbles, pretending they were lollies. I met her mother, "Ole-Great-Nanna," when I was very small, but most of my impressions are from stories Nanna told me. Her mother took her out of school and sent her to look after an elderly woman to earn money for the family. Nanna's repeated stories were often a lament of what could have been; her life, in her eyes, seemed to have been arrested when she was a teenager. She wasn't able to finish school or go to college, and she never spoke of any other opportunity to find a way to achieve what she wanted to achieve in life. Instead she stayed up until 4:00 a.m. most nights, watched a lot of television, and did crossword puzzles. Her house was dusty, and the long vacated kids' bedrooms were piled high with items she hoarded for when she moved into a better house.

She was a binge eater, and this doesn't seem surprising to me considering her relationship with food during her childhood and teens in the Depression years. She said the boys didn't like her because she was stick thin; they liked more voluptuous women during that time.

That made sense to me too—that our culture would promote body types that were hard to attain in whichever time women live.

Nanna became fat after bearing children, and later she had type 2 diabetes and heart problems. She died in her seventies immediately after a quadruple heart bypass surgery. I don't remember exactly when she was diagnosed with diabetes, but I think it was when she was in her fifties, as I remember her taking a pill at each meal when I still lived at home.

When it comes to the generations of women in my family, I can't talk about fatness without talking about mental illness and eating disorders. I know that's not the case for many fat women, but it is in my family. The women on both sides of my family have had husbands with a range of mental illnesses and also abusive behaviour—including war-related PTSD, valium addiction, alcoholism, eating disorders, anger, physical abuse, and fat shaming. The women have experienced eating disorders, borderline personality disorder, obsessive compulsive disorder, social anxiety, panic attacks, depression, agoraphobia, and internalized fat hatred. None of my family has had much medical treatment, so this has affected their children in the form of physical and emotional abuse. My sister and I developed eating disorders, but it's hard to pinpoint when these started. I remember hoarding and binging on restricted foods from the age of four or five. In a family full of binge-eating disorders and bulimia, it was a way of life as a child and teenager. Dieting from the age of eight only worsened the cycle of binging and severe food restriction.

While Nanna was alive, she had shut-in tendencies and didn't have any friends. She hated her thin body, and later in life, she hated her fat body, her pendulous breasts, and her back rolls. When I was a child, she would get dressed in front of me, and walk around in a bra and underwear, but as she did so, she would criticize her body—she called herself a "fat thing" and ugly. The only time I was exposed to fat women's bodies as a child was when they had hate piled on them.

Mum

My mum has never been one to spend much money on dieting. Years ago when I went on HerbaLife and Weight Watchers, she disapproved, not because she didn't want me drinking meal replacement milkshakes or adding up points after every meal. She disapproved because it cost money to go on those diet schemes.

Mum always chose local and low-cost weight loss schemes. I don't remember the name of the one she went to when I was around four years old. Sometimes she took me, and I sat in the corner and coloured in farm animals. I loved farm animals. Pigs were my favourite because my uncle had piglets on his farm, and they were charming little doglike creatures. I don't remember much about being at this weight loss club, except that the women had hats to pin reward brooches onto, and I remember the week mum put on weight. She had to stand up at the front, put on a pig snout, and sing the piggy song. I don't remember my reaction at the time, but I internalized fat hatred over the years of exposure to various ways of hating a fat body.

I have had maybe ten weight-related discussions with my mother over the last few years, although we have stopped now, and don't speak of it. In these discussions I said things like:

You can't control your body or the outcome of healthy behaviours.

I'm not willing to eat fruit for lunch and drink only three glasses of wine a year like you do.

When you say, "It'd be good if you could just get a little bit off," it feels like you're saying, "You're ugly, unhealthy, and I don't accept you the way you are."

Please stop telling me to lose weight.

I think I'm always going to be fat, unless my body decides without me to do something differently.

You've been brainwashed by Dad who told you to lose weight so many times as I grew up.

You're not listening to me.

Studies show that most people who diet to lose weight can't keep more than five percent of their body weight off for more than three years.

Yes, you keep it off, because it is the focus of every day of your life.

What are you looking at? (After getting the up-and-down appraisal).

Don't comment on my weight ever again. Don't look at how much cake I cut.

Don't tell me about your weight loss. This is the definition of "we have to agree to disagree."

I'm screaming through thick glass, and she sees me in pain and is confused. Why am I in pain? She can't hear me. It's every pivotal emotional reaction I had growing up, playing over and over again in a loop. But now I turn away, and let her bang her head against her chosen brick wall.

A few years ago, I agreed to go to the gym with my mum. I wanted to be healthier than I had been, so I wanted to exercise. I could have just walked my dog each day, but I wanted to be able to walk into spaces that scared me and then to conquer them. I am afraid of gyms and swimming pools—any institution of sport or fitness. I can stare at a wall for an hour, willing myself to go to the gym, and my body just will not move. So I often need someone to go with. At first, I felt weak because I needed this support. I would repeat what my grandmother told me: "You have as much right to be in this world as anyone else." Low self-esteem travelled down the maternal family tree. Obviously, Nanna repeated that to herself throughout her life.

I was at the gym, and I got off the bike to go to the grinder machine. My mum was telling Michael, the gym instructor, about the scheme her weight loss group was running. I heard, "So, if you put on weight, you lose a leg. Then, at the end of the competition, the person with the most limbs left wins fifty dollars. I'm a lifer, so I can go a kilogram either side of my goal weight without losing a leg."

Obviously, I was confused. I asked her what she meant, and she said, "We all get an octopus and a leg is lopped off each week that we put on weight. The person with the most legs at the end wins the fifty dollars."

I pictured a lot of rotten, stinking squid being hauled around every week, which was actually a better image than the amateur human amputations I had previously pictured. I then realized they were probably going to use soft toys. Now, I wonder if they used cardboard cut-outs of octopi, coloured in by grandchildren.

I almost cried in the gym when I heard her talk about the scheme because I thought, *you're still there. You're still putting that pig nose on.*

Hell, you metaphorically wear the pig's nose around everywhere you go.

I'd like to say I laughed because it may make this story funnier. Adults—old people, as my mum put it—cut legs off soft toys with such inevitability. Maybe they kept the legs. Maybe once the winner was announced and got the fifty dollars (a diet group where you can make money is pretty unique), they sewed the legs back on.

Yes, that's what I'll go with. Everyone had an intact reminder of their massacre and several kilos of weight loss. Everyone lived happily ever after, especially the octopi. Until everyone except my mum put the weight back on.

Daughter

At Easter time, I took my two-year-old daughter to a chocolate cafe so we could have a drink and a chocolate and buy gifts for relatives. We entered and there was chocolate from floor to ceiling. I looked down and realized I'd been expecting her to act like she was in *Charlie and the Chocolate Factory* and be in absolute awe. Instead, she said, "Let's get Daddy one of these." She then chose a chocolate lollipop and a small hot chocolate drink. As a child, I would have been in awe of such an illicit substance displayed in excess, but after half her chocolate, she asked to go to the park and play on the swings.

My daughter, Rosie, measured in the ninety-fifth percentile size-wise when I was pregnant. I don't know if it was genetic or partly due to my type 2 diabetes. I was able to keep my HbA1c, which measures sugar levels in the blood over three months, at 5.5 throughout pregnancy. This is the same level a pregnant woman without diabetes would expect her HbA1c to be. However, there are still more fluctuations in blood sugar with diabetes, so Rosie was probably exposed to more highs and lows than other fetuses. I kept my blood sugars at that level by channelling the old-obsessive-dieting-guilt-ridden-Jenny and measured my blood eight times a day, injected insulin four or five times a day, and ate mainly low-GI foods. I had a supportive partner, and high-quality medical care from an obstetrician and endocrinologist that didn't fat shame me. In fact, the obstetrician said that Rosie was probably large because both Nick and I were tall. Whether or not that was the case, I was impressed that she didn't just make assumptions about my fatness being the cause.

Toward the end of the pregnancy, Rosie wasn't getting enough nutrition and her growing had slowed. I said to the obstetrician, "She's starving in there," and she responded, "We don't think of it like that." But I agreed to an induction at thirty-eight weeks, which resulted in a traumatic and long labour followed by an emergency C-section. Rosie was born in the fifteenth percentile.

In the following weeks, she emptied my breasts of milk, and I pumped after every feed in an effort to make more. Apart from formula in the first few days at the hospital, I managed to feed her exclusively breastmilk for the first six weeks, but it took sixteen hours in an armchair, feeding and pumping. I was exhausted, only left the house for a walk each day, and showered every three or four days. A GP friend of mine visited and said, "Formula isn't poison—just give her a bottle." From five weeks until five months of age, she had breastmilk and one bottle of formula a day. It wasn't the slippery slope I was warned about that breastmilk production decreases as formula is used. But I continued to pump and feed, and hold myself to a breastfeeding ransom. I rarely enjoyed time out of the house. I had imagined going to cafes with her, but because of my fatness and bust size, I couldn't find a maternity bra that would fit me—not in Australia and not online (after days of searching). I should have paid the three hundred dollars quoted to me to have one tailor made.

Rosie was growing exponentially. By her eight-month-old maternal health visit, she was back in the ninety-fifth percentile. That didn't surprise me, as my research into dieting (or food restriction or starvation) showed that the body will attempt to gain back what it lost, plus more. But the nurse suggested I cut out the formula and put Rosie on a diet. I'm not sure what effect it had that I am fat—whether a growing baby with a slim mother would have attracted the same attention. I ignored the suggestion and fed Rosie according to her hunger and satiety cues. I had done three years of a mindful moderate eating program in treatment for my own binge-eating disorder, and I observed hunger cues in Rosie carefully. She is a strong-willed baby and child. There were a few times when I wasn't paying attention and was poking my nipple at her mouth, and she would clamp her lips shut and refuse to budge. I'd look down, and she'd look up at me, mouth clamped shut, as if to say "I'm not hungry." I trust her cues.

As a toddler, her father and I have seen her leave one spoonful of chocolate ice cream in her bowl. This has happened with lollipops, gummy snakes, French fries, and all of the foods I used to binge eat—those foods I was raised to see as illicit, harmful, or bad. We have incorporated them into her diet successfully, and that is what I call healthy eating. We don't endorse schools that ban sweets from their cafeterias. I believe that learning to eat high-calorie or junk food in moderation is a skill, and removing those foods from a house leaves the child without the skills to eat them in moderation from the beginning of their life.

Rosie has a healthier relationship with food than I ever had as a child. I hope this continues, but I worry that it will change when she is exposed to primary school and the warped antiobesity messages start affecting her and when her classmates develop eating disorders around her. At this stage, Rosie hasn't been exposed to a relationship between food and body size. Well, perhaps she has at my mum's house, but I hope that influence is low compared to all the time she spends with us and at childcare, where there seems to be a good attitude toward children and food.

Recently, the doctor weighed Rosie to check a dosage of a medication for croup. At home, I had measured her height and marked it on the wall, as is tradition. Out of curiosity, I entered the measurements into an online child BMI calculator and it spat out the result "obese." I was shocked. She isn't petite; she's fairly stocky, with chubby thighs and a small belly, so I'm not sure why I'm shocked because there is such a narrow range for what is considered a healthy body size. I will try to ensure she is never subjected to a health check or a school program that weighs her with shame attached. I see the strength of fat stigma. I worry about whether she will be teased for having a fat mum, whether I will be blamed if she stays in the obese category, or whether she will soak up the information she is fed about health at school and come home and tell me I should lose weight. I have considered delaying her entry to school to delay her exposure to antiobesity messages, or home schooling her for the first year or two, again, to delay her exposure to these messages.

I also try to build her body admiration and respect, and I started talking to Rosie when she was about two years old about all the things her body can do. I've been massaging her several times a week since she was a baby to encourage a positive relationship with her body, especially after she had spinal taps and IVs in her hands as a one-month-old. Now when we massage her legs I say, "It's great all the things your legs and body can do," and she says, "They run, and walk, and jump, and climb, and crawl, and swim—when you teach me to swim. I want to learn!" This stems from research I read about girls that value what their body can do, and not just what it looks like (Abbott; Abbott and Barber). I also said to her, "The most amazing thing my body ever did was grow and carry you inside me and then feed you with milk." She looked very self-satisfied about that.

We enjoy dancing together, and, recently, we danced naked in the lounge room after we'd shared a shower. She watched how my body moved, which parts jiggled and said, "Will I have a double belly when I grow up?" I had previously explained to her that I call my type of stomach a double belly, and I said, "I'm not sure; everyone has a different body. You might have a round belly, or a double belly, or a flat belly."

The most recent positive body play is when I was in a silly mood and I lifted my top and did a dance with my upper belly, using some belly dance moves I'd learned years before, and I sang, "Bada boom, bada boom, bada boom boom boom." She now asks to talk to Bada Boom, who speaks in a gruff voice, and enjoys bouncing our bellies against each other. I initiated that after seeing fat activist and scholar Charlotte Cooper's "Chubsters" short film, where she bangs bellies with other fatties. After I kissed Rosie's belly when I changed her diaper she said, "Careful, Bada Boom is full." We had had porridge and strawberries just before this.

Coda

Often in the fat-acceptance movement, I read about moving from fat hatred to fat love. When I reflect on the generations of mothers on my maternal side, I see a transition from fat hatred to fat play—a fun and kindness to the body. I enjoy dressing up and having massages and swimming in a bathing suit. I'm not sure if that translates directly as body love because it takes conscious effort to fight the antifat messages I grew up with, and still face in our culture. And it's complex to try to love a body that has been physically abused growing up and that has suffered a severe diet-and-binge eating disorder. I'm not sure the opposite of hatred is love, but I'm hoping the body respect that Rosie experiences with her fat mother gives her a strong foundation to fight the antifat messages to come. After having witnessed so much fat hatred in the women of my family, I feel that caring for and having fun with my body, with my daughter as a witness, is transformative for me.

Works Cited

Abbott, Bree. "Teaching Girls to Prioritise Function Over Form for Better Body Image". *The Conversation*, 5 Feb. 2013, theconversation. com/teaching-girls-to-prioritise-function-over-form-for-better-body-image-11620 Accessed 13 Aug. 2018.

Abbott, Bree, and Bonnie Barber, "Embodied Image: Gender Differences in Functional and Aesthetic Body Image among Australian Adolescents." *Body Image*, vol. 7, no. 1, 2010, pp. 22-31.

Cooper, Charlotte. "Chubsters." *YouTube*, 2009. www.youtube. com/watch?v=AHnCpVo5Lnk. Accessed 13 Aug. 2018.

Chapter Thirteen

Exoskeleton

Sherezada Windham-Kent

I was tired of feeling like a frumpy stay-at-home mom, of living in plain knit shirts and old jeans. I decided I was going to dress up a little—on a weekday, no less—just for the sake of looking cute. I had woken up earlier than usual, and as my husband and two-year-old snoozed, I made my transformation. I blow-dried my short hair, and carefully applied my new silvery-grey eyeshadow. I even decided to give my silver *Star Wars* lipstick a try for the first time. I assembled as cute an outfit as I could muster out of my wardrobe, and accessorized with big dangly earrings and a fun choker I'd picked up at a plus-size clothing swap the weekend before. When I looked in the mirror, I was thrilled with the results. I didn't look like the tired, overextended mother of a toddler. I looked like a fun, fashionable person. Like those gorgeous fashionistas—no, *fat*shionistas—that made up much of my social media feeds. Now I was one of those body-positive warriors, ready to take on the world.

I was so pleased that I snapped a selfie—the first I had taken solo in months. In fact, it looked so good that I decided that it was time to follow in the footsteps of some of my plus-size fashion heroes—model Tess Holliday, singer Beth Ditto, fashion blogger Isabell Decker—and create an Instagram account of body positivity. This selfie would be the first post, but there would be more, of course. I was going to create a whole series of selfies, add my voice, and my body, to the self-love revolution. #fatbabe #effyourbeautystandards #hotmama

I was glowing as I got my toddler son ready for the day. I plopped him into his bath as I did every morning, and sat with him in the bathroom as he played in the water. I was so busy connecting to other body-positive bloggers on Instagram that I didn't notice at first when my son's cheerful chirping turned into strained grunting. By the time I looked up from my phone, it was too late. There he was, lying on his tummy, growing a tail.

Never, in his entire life, had he pooped in the tub before, so I had no previous programming for this. I froze for a full second before mom instinct kicked in, and I leapt up to try to scoop him up and get him to the toilet before he finished. No such luck, though. By the time I reached him, his little present was floating freely among his colourful bath toys.

Bath time became the pool scene from *Caddyshack*—scrambling, splashing, and frantically pulling him out of the water while mentally screaming, "Doody! There's doody in the bathtub!" For his part, my son was unfazed, wrapped in his towel, watching with mild curiosity as mommy tried not to completely freak out. I couldn't figure out what to do. How could I clean my son if the tub was still a mess, but how could I clean the tub if I had to watch my son? I tried calling for backup from my husband, but he was already in the other shower, deaf to my high-pitched cries for assistance. I was on my own.

Off came the dangly earrings, the choker, and the cute top. I shoved my curled hair back away from my face as I hovered over the tub, rescuing all the toys for a deep-clean later. That only left one more thing—the offending matter itself. In my panicked state, I could only think of one way to remove it. I picked it up with my bare hands and dropped it into the toilet.

As I vigorously scrubbed my hands in the bathroom sink with soap and scalding hot water, I caught a glimpse of myself in the mirror, still wearing that gorgeous silver eyeshadow and matching lipstick. My stomach knotted. Who did I think I was? I wasn't a body-positive warrior or a fatshionista. I was just a frazzled, overtired mother of a toddler who had just reminded her of what her life was really about these days—cleaning poop. #momlife #wtf #fml

When so much of the current body-positive movement seems to centre on visibility—through fashion and online presence—how does someone who doesn't have the time or capacity for such engagement still feel like a part of the movement? This question has added an extra layer for me to navigate on my own journey of radical self-acceptance, and has led to a bit of a love/hate relationship with the "fatshion" component of body-positive activism.

Don't get me wrong. In itself, fatshion is amazing. I think it's incredibly important to increase visibility of all marginalized body types. My culture, American culture, is flooded with (over-Photo-shopped) images of young, slim, light-skinned, able-bodied, cis-gendered people, and I believe that we need more positive images of older, fat, racialized, disabled, and trans* folks to help us not only accept each other's differences, but our own. Plus-size fashion blogs and Tumblr feeds are great for this. DapperQ, Fat Girl Flow, Dressing Outside the Box, Fuck Yeah Fat Positive, and Chubstr are some of my favorites. I love seeing all that out-and-proud body positivity: teen girls showing off their VBOs (visible belly outlines), genderfluid pioneers rocking skater skirts and stubble. As a fat, biracial woman, it's remarkably healing to see big folks of colour looking so visibly fashionable, and it gives me hope that we're slowly but surely starting to move towards a more size-acceptant culture.

However, there is a disconnect between what I see on my screens and what's happening in my real life. I can spend hours scrolling through Ashley Nell Tipton's or Rebel Wilson's new fashion lines, creating fantasy ensembles in my mind, but when I face my actual closet, all that inspiration evaporates as reality sets in. Gone are the cute skull-print sundresses, my red suede jacket, my Gibson-swirl Fluevogs. Now, most of my wardrobe consists of comfortable, plain knit tops, practical sneakers, and jeans that have never quite recovered from when they doubled as maternity pants.

This is the crux of my dilemma: fashion is not meant to be practical. "One should either be a work of art, or wear a work of art," according to Oscar Wilde (177). Fashion is an expression of the inner self—or of the desired self—whether you're wearing high-dollar fashion-week frocks or street-level thrifted ensembles. It's a way to dream in fabric and paint, using your body as the canvas.

Early parenthood, however, is a realm completely dominated by the practical. Infants and toddlers don't care what you're wearing. In fact, they don't care if you've eaten all day, had enough sleep, or are in the midst of an existential crisis. Their needs are simple and absolute: food, sleep, cleanliness, and attention. Constant, unending attention. When my son was a baby, I barely had enough energy to get to the grocery store with him, never mind spend hours combing racks of thrift store clothes for that perfect "score," or modifying an old t-shirt into a cute DIY top. I was neither a work of art nor wearing works of art. I was a new mom. I didn't have room in my life for art.

Whenever I voiced my frustration to more experienced moms, I'd get a sympathetic smile and a pat on the shoulder: "There will be time later—for fashion, for art, for everything—once the little one is older and doesn't need you so much." Although deep down I knew they were right, at that point in my life, I felt the most vulnerable about my appearance, especially my fatness. I used to be terrified of being seen as the stereotypical "sloppy fat person" if I showed up to the grocery store in leggings and no makeup. On a slim woman, it's an admirably low-key look. On a fat woman, it's a sign that she's given up on herself.

I have spent years—most of my life, in fact—fighting that very perception. Just because I'm fat doesn't mean I don't care about my appearance. In fact, I care all the more for it. Back in my youth in the late nineties and early aughts, fashion had been a form of armour for me—a protective colouration, like how the monarch butterfly warns predators of its toxicity with its brightly coloured wings. I tricked my high school bullies with my punk-goth look, deflecting their taunts of my size and onto my scary style. People stopped whispering "fatty" and "butterball" when I passed in the halls. It became "witch" or "vampire," which suited me just fine. Witches and vampires were sexy and dangerous, as anyone who's read Anne Rice or Bram Stoker knows. More importantly, it was a mantle I'd taken on myself. No one had forced it upon me because of my body shape or genetics. It was the first time I truly understood the power of fashion in creating one's outward self.

In college, my style became more than armour; it was a form of political expression. My patent leather combat boots, flowing black skirts, and embroidered Mexican dresses became my uniform as I navigated UC Berkeley's film studies, women's studies, and Chicano studies departments. Through my network of feminist friends, I discovered life-changing books like Marilyn Wann's *Fat!So?*, Naomi Wolf's *The Beauty Myth*, and Hanne Blank's *Big, Big Love*. I felt like I had found my true cause—the fat activism movement—and I made it the core of my creative work. My final project for a film studies class was a short, performative documentary about my journey toward size acceptance. I even began creating a hand-written zine (it was the early aughts, everyone had a zine) titled *Gordita*, which was going to be my size-positive manifesto. By the time I graduated college, I had reached an apex of personal strength, and I had the stylish armour to prove it. Hell, I had so much armour I even had dress armor now. If social media had been a thing then, you bet I would've been flooding my Instagram with all of my creative outfits. #fuckyourfascistbeautystandards

Things began to change as soon as I left the bubble of academe. I was able to keep the core of my style as I moved through the Bay Area nonprofit workforce, but I had to be a bit more muted to be professional. I traded fishnets for black slacks, heeled boots for commuter-friendly oxfords. My armour functioned the same way it had in school by helping me surpass the trope of being just "the fat girl in the office." Instead, I was the "quirky one" with her dark makeup, leather cuff bracelets, and all-black business-casual wardrobe. I was *NCIS*'s sharp, goth forensics scientist Abby instead of *How I Met Your Mother*'s plus-size punching bag Patrice. Never mind that I would never fit into Abby's size XS lab coat. I felt stronger, braver, more secure, even as I moved from one job to the next.

I learned the hard way, though, that even the best armour can be broken by the right blow. When my husband and I survived a near-fatal car crash two days after Christmas in 2008, I was left with a semipermanent knee injury. I walked with a cane for months, and met weekly with a team of physical therapists for over a year. In that time, fashion had to give way to function. Doctor's orders—and my own body's demands—dictated that I replace my cute shoes with supportive sneakers. I felt like Frankenstein's monster clomping around in those thick-soled monstrosities. My wardrobe had to shift to accommodate the change, and gradually more jeans and practical knit tops began to filter in to my wardrobe. I lost my defenses a piece at a time, and with them, much of my confidence. It didn't help that my career came to an abrupt end when the organization I was working for at the time closed. By the time I hit my thirties, I had no job, a long-term injury, and no armour of personal style to hide behind. I felt naked, exposed—just another fat woman lumbering around in ugly clothes.

That feeling went on for years, and even followed me into early motherhood. Although I was truly thrilled to have a child—and more than a little relieved that my plus-size body had carried a healthy, uneventful pregnancy—I hadn't been mentally prepared for the impact new motherhood would have on my already fragile sense of self. My family's limited finances at the time kept me from being able to buy clothes and shoes to replace the ones that I had outgrown in my pregnancy, so I wore my maternity clothes and nursing bras well into my son's second year. My hair fell out in clumps thanks to the loss of pregnancy hormones, and makeup was pointless when I would just cry it off in a spell of postpartum depression. Even jewelry and accessories were out of the question, as anyone who's had their earring ripped out by a curious baby can tell you.

I felt completely naked. Vulnerable. My body still suffered lingering pains from the car crash, which were exacerbated by carrying my hundredth-percentile-sized son around. Anyone who looked at me could plainly see how big I was. There was no way to deflect attention from my fatness anymore. At the park, I'd overhear slim, stylish yoga moms compare workout notes, talking about how they were "losing that baby weight," and I'd want to hide behind the play structure. I had been fat before my pregnancy, I had been fat during my pregnancy, and I was still fat. I felt like the anomaly at the playground, the elephant in the room.

Of course, my eventual solution was to drink the Kool-Aid and try to lose weight (again) to "take control" of my life. I got a gym membership and started riding the exercise bike twice a week. At first, it had just been to move my body, but as the pounds began to come off, I pushed myself harder. My body pushed back, though, and my old car-crash injuries flared up. I was forced off the bike, back into physical therapy, and into the realization that there was nothing I could do to change being fat—except to finally accept it.

Although I'd talked a fine game in college about size acceptance and self-love, I'd never truly internalized my own message. My armour had been just a hollow shell. Deep down, I'd always hated myself for being fat, wondering what would happen if I'd just worked a little harder, ate a little less, really committed myself to weight loss. Well, now I had my answer: it led to injury, deepened depression, and disappointment. The truth was I had always been big and I would probably always be big. It was time to learn to be okay with that.

As my old copies of *Fat!So?* and *Big, Big Love* had been packed away with the majority of my books when my home office became a nursery, I turned to the Internet. There, I found the body-positive movement still going, actively growing and thriving. I learned about Linda Bacon's

Health at Every Size movement, Virgie Tovar and her #LoseHate NotWeight Babecamp, and Substantia Jones's photo-activism campaign, the Adiposity Project. I read, I learned, and I remembered what had drawn me to size acceptance in the first place: the radical notion that all people, including fat people, were deserving of dignity, respect, and love. That meant me, too.

At my husband's urging, I ventured out alone to a release party in San Francisco for Jes Baker's book *Things No One Will Tell Fat Girls: A Handbook for Unapologetic Living.* I showed up late and had to sit behind a rack of t-shirts in the bookstore, but as soon as Jes introduced her first guest reader—Sonya Renee Taylor of *The Body Is Not an Apology*—I was transported. Here, in the flesh were so many of those body-positive warriors I admired, and some new ones I had not yet discovered. They spoke candidly about being fat, racialized, and/or queer in a world of thin, white, straight privilege, and about the work they did to combat fatphobia, racism, and homophobia (both internalized and institutionalized). Some shared their personal journeys toward radical self-love, and as they spoke, I began to wonder what it would feel like to share that feeling—to not only accept my body the way it was but to love it, including my flabby belly, my wounded knee, my breasts that had never produced enough milk to feed my son. What would it be like to unlearn the years of internalized hatred, of self-loathing?

I'd like to say that I instantly fell in radical love with myself in that moment, like some offbeat meet-cute in a movie: girl meets self, cue sparks. I wish it had been so easy. It's been months of work with readings, workshops, and therapy sessions, and at this point, I'm proud to say that I've become my own friend, at least. I appreciate my body for what, and who, it's created, where it's taken me, and what it's survived.

Part of this healing journey has definitely involved clothing. As our financial situation improved, I began prioritizing buying basics for myself—a properly fitting bra here, a pair of cute (yet comfortable) sneakers there. Birthday and holiday gift cards for Torrid and Lane Bryant got me some updated looks. I decided to cut off my thinned hair into a nice, short style. I can even wear some of my jewelry again, since my son is past his impulsive grabbing stage. Although I wouldn't consider myself on trend, or cultivating a look anymore, I definitely feel more confident and put together than I have in a long time.

The biggest turning point came when I attended my first plus-size clothing swap, appropriately titled "Fattyland." For years, I had been holding on to so many of my old pieces of armour—that clothing I had to stop wearing when my body began to change because of either injury or childbearing. I'd clung to this fantasy, as so many other people do, that perhaps I would fit into them again or find occasion to wear them. The truth was I didn't need them anymore. I had moved past that armour and the illusion of the protection it had brought. My armour hadn't saved me from school bullying, from prejudice in the workplace, or from my worst tormentor—myself.

I traded in that old armour and watched it go to new owners with a sort of bittersweet release. In exchange, I took home the potential for new expression, a chance at exploring new styles for the fun of it: a red polka-dotted dress, a pair of skinny jeans, a silver choker.

This brings me back to that moment alone in the bathroom a few days later, when I was scrubbing my son's poop out of the tub while wearing that same silver choker and matching lipstick. How was I ever going to make this new method of self-expression mesh with the mundanity of early motherhood? When part of being a fat activist seemed to mean wearing lots of cute clothes, snapping selfies, and being outwardly visible in defiance of conventional beauty norms, how could I participate when the reality of my life made it all but impossible?

Perhaps I had been going about this all the wrong way.

Fat activism is more than just a social media hashtag, more than just a series of cute selfies. It's a radical shift in mentality. It's internal as well as external, a battle for self-acceptance as well as a struggle for societal change. Sure, dressing my body nicely is definitely an act of self-love, but so is giving myself permission to go to the store in an old t-shirt and no makeup. I don't owe my appearance to strangers, especially when my priority is to care for the wellbeing of a messy, active little human.

Without the armour of fashion to hide behind, I'm being forced to grow an actual exoskeleton, forged from my own knowledge and lived experiences. It's not just about the clothes; it's about what I do inside of them. I can still be a body-positive warrior in old sweats while pushing my son on the swing at the park. I may still be the elephant in the room, but elephants are tough mothers—big, strong, and smart. Not to be messed with.

Right now, the idea of high-profile internet visibility isn't appealing. Much of it is genuine fear—read the comments section of many fat activists' blogs and you'll see the parade of hatred and fatphobia that follows them like a dark comet tail. *Dances with Fat*'s Ragen Chastain has so many haters that they've created an entire Reddit page and blog devoted to tearing her down. There's a whole world of ugly backlash out there, and at this point in my life, I don't have the capacity to welcome such open antagonism. Not for just posting a picture of myself in a pretty dress.

It makes me see these young, online fatshionistas in a new light. Perhaps those crop tops, body-con dresses, and candy-bright hair colours serve the same function for them as my flowing black skirts and spiked collars had for me in the past—as armour. Armor for this generation of body-positive warriors trying to navigate a toxic world, still struggling to find peace in the flesh they've been taught by society to hate. Each cute outfit is a deflection, each picture posted a defiant middle finger to the bullies. It gives them courage, a sense of solidarity, and builds strength for the real war within themselves. One photo is just a selfie, but a thousand is a revolution.

Until the day I'm brave enough to add my images, I've found my own low-profile ways to be active in the fat-activism movement: reading books and blogs, attending events and performances, supporting body positive businesses, and now finally writing about my own experiences. Most importantly, I'm raising my son to be a body-positive feminist (ideals that both his father and I hold) in the hopes he'll carry these lessons with him as he grows to adulthood.

These days, my favourite selfies are the ones in which my son joins me, hamming it up for the camera with his toothy, three-year-old grin. I'm not wearing any makeup, and I'm usually in a hoodie with peanut-butter smears on it. I'm smiling, though, wide and bright. Never mind my crooked teeth, my double chin, my lack of makeup. In those moments with him, I am at peace with myself, and in love with my life just the way it is. #bodyacceptance #motherhood

Works Cited

Wilde, Oscar. *Complete Works.* Vol 6, National Library Company, 1909.

Additional Links

Adipositivity Project: adipositivity.com

The Body is Not an Apology: thebodyisnotanapology.com

Chubstr: chubstr.com

Dances With Fat: danceswithfat.wordpress.com/blog

DapperQ: dapperq.com

Dressing Outside the Box: dressingoutsidethebox.net

Fat Girl Flow: fatgirlflow.com

Fuck Yeah Fat Positive: fuckyeahfatpositive.tumblr.com

Health at Every Size: haescommunity.com

Lose Hate Not Weight: virgietovar.com

Smiling Emma Day

Chapter Fourteen

The Fat of the Matter: Fat Activist Parenting in Fatphobic Times

Judy Verseghy

The project of creating the ideal neoliberal subject begins at pre-conception and lasts a lifetime. Genetic counselling, maternal vitamins, Mozart played through earphones placed on either side of the belly, motherhood manuals, careful exercise, and dietary choices throughout pregnancy—all of these come together as part of the project of creating the perfect citizen. One who embodies characteristics valued in the current neoliberal and patriarchal climate, including self-sufficiency, restraint, strong work ethic, independence, competence, capability, and un-wavering commitment to the ongoing project of self-management (physical, emotional, psychological, and material).

The pressure on mothers to create idealized citizens is, at times, almost unbearable. We are tasked with making a multitude of minute yet understood as critical decisions that will shape the lives of our children for years to come: breast vs. bottle, infant swim classes vs. infant yoga, French immersion vs. English schooling, gymnastics vs. hockey, or piano vs. violin. As part of the project of citizen making, we must make these decisions. The stakes are high. After all, everyone wants their child to have the best possible chance of doing well in life. Since doing well is defined, at its most basic level, as independence via financial stability and maintaining a healthy body, providing children with cultural capital via early and rigorous indoctrination into the neoliberal ethos can have a significant impact on their life-long success.

Not surprisingly, body management represents a significant percentage of work required by the neoliberal person-project, and the well-managed body is seen as representing the aforementioned values— so much so that food consumption has come to take on aspects of morality in our culture. So-called good food is not heavily processed, is low calorie, and is natural. It should keep you slim. By consuming these good foods, we become good citizen subjects who care about our bodies and what we put into them, who view our health as something that can be controlled through careful intake and purposeful output, and who are self-regulating, thoughtful, and self-contained. Interestingly, in a culture where material consumption is prized, consumption in the form of (over)eating and eating bad foods is vilified, as it threatens the success of the body project (Guthman and DuPuis, 445).

Women are hit particularly hard with this body management requirement thanks to the intersecting of neoliberal and patriarchal values that collude to create untenably narrow realms of acceptability for women's embodiments. By maintaining slim figures and so-called attractive bodies, women can achieve success on both neoliberal and patriarchal fronts. The pressure for women to make good body-management choices is ubiquitous; it asserts its presence via media and advertising, news articles, social pressure, and the medical industrial complex. The diet industry relies on this pressure to coerce women to buy into the myth that diets work and will bring health and happiness to the dieter, although evidence overwhelmingly suggests they are ineffective (Mann et al., 220). Gyms also rely on this rhetoric to sell memberships. And these two aspects of bodily management— consumption and expulsion—work together in women's daily lives, as evidenced by the overwhelming number of women I have heard in my lifetime who have justified eating a cookie by mentioning their earlier Zumba class—using their prior "good" body management behaviour to justify their consumption of a "bad" food.

Mothers of course are tasked with, and judged on, managing not only their own bodies but those of their children (Zivkovic et al., 377). Rhetoric surrounding the "childhood obesity crisis" has resulted in increased discussion around the morality of raising fat children, and has inspired a plethora of fat-shaming advertisements aimed at the mothers of fat children (and even, unfortunately, the children themselves) (Beerman, 24). Stigma around childhood obesity vilifies both fat children (and children perceived as fat) and their mothers—some of whom may also be fat—and compounds everyday microaggressions aimed at fat people. As a fat mother to a (perceived as) fat child, I have personally experienced discrimination at the hands of other parents, educators, and medical professionals. Statements disguised as concern are spewed from the lips of others who were not asked their opinions, but they chose to give them anyway because mothers and keepers of fat bodies are viewed as being in constant need of public opinion for their own sake and the sake of their children.

Even as a fat activist these comments and the overarching societal disdain held for fat mothers and fat children can be difficult to navigate. Internalized fatphobia can hide deep within the soul, even when trying to disentangle oneself from its clutches. Reprogramming my own thinking to no longer see myself as weak willed, unattractive, and unable to make good choices takes work—less work than it did years ago, but work nonetheless. It is a long and sometimes difficult process.

My experiences with my own body and my fat politics bleed into my parenting choices and interactions with my children, who also struggle against damaging antifat narratives. Societally, we have made strides in a variety of forms of discrimination, although we are still far from ideal in any way. Yet the fat kid still becomes a social pariah in the schoolyard, on the city streets, and, for some, even in their own home. The psychological damage resulting from trying to exist as a fat kid in a fatphobic society can be life changing. Our fat activist household, then, should be a safe haven against body shaming—a place where my children can be unburdened from the overt and covert commentary on their bodies and selves. For the most part, it is.

My children and I spend time, almost daily, working through fatphobia together, yet the pressure to be a good mother to good children in the manner espoused by our neoliberal, patriarchal society sometimes creeps in. When I was a fat child, my mother worked to restrict my intake of bad foods and to increase my energy output via soccer and swimming. Although I internalized these efforts as harmful, as an adult, I recognize that she was acting out of love. She tried to shield me from the social, psychological, and potential physical pain of living in a fat body. In response to the hurt I have felt from this form of love, I have not discouraged the consumption of "bad" foods, and although I have encouraged movement, I have not been militant about it. I have never stressed any form of weight loss, and, in fact, I have actively discouraged purposeful weight loss. On occasion, the pressure I feel both as a woman and mother causes me to doubt my convictions. I wonder where my fat-activist stance falls in the context of bringing harm to my children. I question whether my focus on arming them against a fatphobic society instead of encouraging them to work toward more normative bodies will cause them more harm in the end.

But how can it be wrong to teach children to love themselves and their bodies? Or to educate them to be critical of the messages they hear seeking to make women's bodies as small as possible? How can it be wrong to prioritize their mental health and to arm them against hatred?

In the end, I don't think it can.

Ultimately, bodies are fluid. They change, they age, and they become (increasingly) disabled. A focus on maintaining a particular type of body creates an unsustainable source of satisfaction, if such a body is even achievable. But the critical thinking and self-love skills I am teaching my children can be carried with them over their hopefully long and fulfilling lives.

Both my mother and I seek to protect our kids' health via the use of food, although we take completely different routes. Oftentimes, it seems there are no right answers, as it often is once mothers divorce themselves from an overarching societal narrative. And sometimes I mess up, just as my mother sometimes messed up. But, like her, I keep trying to do my best in the face of immense societal pressure, and I simply hope for the best in the end.

Works Cited

Beerman, R. "Containing Fatness: Bodies, Motherhood, and Civic Identity in Contemporary U.S. Culture." Dissertation, University of Wisconsin-Milwaukee, 2015.

Guthman, J., and M. DuPuis. "Embodying Neoliberalism: Economy, Culture, and the Politics of Fat." *Environment and Planning D: Society and Space*, vol. 24, 2006, pp. 427-88.

Mann, T., et al. "Medicare's Search for Effective Obesity Treatments: Diets Are Not the Answer." *American Psychology*, vol. 62, no. 3, 2007, pp. 220-33.

Zivkovic, T., et al. "In the Name of the Child: The Gendered Politics of Childhood Obesity." *Journal of Sociology*, vol. 46, no. 4, 2010, pp. 375-92.

Chapter Fifteen

Passing It On

Kimberly Dark

Becoming Mother in Cultural Context

My mother-in-law already thought I was too fat and didn't mind telling me so. She said being fat and pregnant was going to harm the baby. She commented on how much fatter I was getting as the baby grew. I gained eighty pounds during that pregnancy, so she was right. Of course, when the baby was born healthy at nine pounds four ounces, she claimed her own genetic material had saved him from the harm I'd done as a fat vegetarian. This made me an incomprehensible oxymoron of course—fat and vegetarian—but no need to revise her ideas. She remained sure of everything. She was also interested in the conformity of my feminine appearance. When she visited the hospital room during my active labour, she said to her son, "Couldn't she put on a little makeup?"

I shrieked from the bed, "Get her out of here!" She and the rest of the family had the good sense to go out to dinner while the baby was being born.

Contrast her views to the response my body received from women during a visit to the Bahamas when I was eight-months pregnant. I was indeed large, but I felt my size meant something significantly different. I experienced women running out of shops to put their hands on my belly and exclaim, again and again, with smiling faces, "You're enormous!" Sometimes they'd add, "What a big healthy baby you're going to have." And then they'd joke with each other and me, saying, "No, she's not having one baby. That's twins!" or "Definitely triplets!"

or "Still a month to go? More than one baby in there for sure!" At first overwhelmed by the attention and unexpected touching, I quickly settled into the happiness my round body evoked.

Even in the U.S., most people treated me more like a pregnant woman than like a fat woman during that time. It was a welcome relief from being generally seen as lazy and overindulgent. Being pregnant is at least creative; there is labour involved and a tangible outcome that is generally thought to be a blessing—so long as one is white, straight, cisgendered, able-bodied, and not poor. This is how my culture understands the productivity of the fat female body. As my white breasts swelled with milk and I carried the new progeny in my fat arms, I was perceived as a fecund part of expansionist America, whereas poorer, browner Americans might be seen as a burden on the nation's brilliance.

Passing It On

He told me years later.

In middle school, he began throwing away the cards and cheques his paternal grandparents sent him at birthdays and Christmas. During college, my son considered changing his last name so that he'd have less connection to them. In addition to being racist, his paternal grandmother in particular just wasn't very nice. My son grew up listening to his father's stories of trying to please her, of her drinking. He had also heard the aforementioned story of her demanding I put on a more pleasing face during childbirth. That's a dramatic story, but I believe there was less gravity in my telling since, she wasn't my mother. She was his grandmother, though, and he felt pain about her cruelty and judgments.

She once told him—when he was about six—that I was going to die an early death because I was too fat. He cried as he told me, and I can imagine how she must've spit the word "fat" because I've seen her do it myself. She was a petite woman, still able to get in my face and look down her nose at me, although she stood a good eight inches shorter than me. She belittled family members directly—no polite talk and withering glances, like my mother offered—about how things should be and how I just didn't measure up.

Joining a new family through marriage is about learning new ways.

I remember once using my husband's cheque at a department store to make a purchase and having the cosmetics counter clerk look at me with recognition based on the name. My mother-in-law shopped there often and had spoken of me, apparently. The clerk said, "Well, you're just as pretty as she said you were. And she brags about how smart you are too!"

My mouth hung open, unable to believe we were speaking of the same person. The clerk repeated her name twice, my husband's name, and my name, before I closed my mouth, nodded and smiled, "Well, isn't that nice to hear."

That's how abuse-centred families do it sometimes, I learned. Close the ranks to protect from the outside, but inside, it's brutal.

My son was raised differently, and he wasn't having it. She was a big meanie, and he refused to visit them anymore. He kept a relationship open with my mother. She's also a white racist, sweet as pie, opinionated and funny, and I noticed how the barbs she threw about bodies slid right off of him. He was Teflon whereas I was fur, matted bloody through time so everything stuck. One night when he was about ten, the three of us played cards while he ate from a box of movie candy in his shirt pocket—the kind of hard-sugary-bits candy that would make my mouth ache. He loved those things, munching as we played. She interjected occasionally, "Ew, I just can't stand to see you eat all that candy." And "Caleb, it's making me sick. It's going to make you sick too." And "You don't want to get fat on all that candy, do you?" And "What can I do to get you to stop eating that candy?" She wrung her hands and gave him the same looks that taught me hot shame and defiant determination as a child.

He just chuckled, unmoved by her remarks. His mind on the game, he'd chirp cheerfully, "I feel fine." And, "I'm not fat, Grandma." And, "Candy is good."

It was all I could do to stay in my chair. I wanted to stand and scream at my mother, "Look at me! Why do you think that kind of shaming works?!"

I felt both triumphant for holding my tongue and a coward for not speaking up on his behalf. He clearly didn't need it though. She had long since stopped looking at my body, lost cause that I was. His was still a soul worth saving.

While I was pregnant, I developed a small jiggly pocket of fat that hung from the bottom of my baby belly. It's still there now, decades later. I had been a certain kind of fat before the pregnancy. Distribution of weight matters. At five foot nine and about 220 pounds and doing six to eight aerobics classes per week and walking often, I was tall, strong, and shaped like a bombshell from another era. I was still "too fat," but the kind of too fat that could be overlooked if a person liked a little extra potato and gravy with that plate of porkchops. I recall once, in Lamaze class, the men and the women being separated to make lists of the pros and cons of the pregnant body. I overheard men commenting on how hot their wives were now that they were getting some soft curves, bigger boobs. My husband commented, "Yeah, she already had great boobs and curves. Now it's getting a little out of hand."

Although I never stopped exercising, those eighty pounds I added during the pregnancy mostly stuck around after the birth. My young adolescent history with food deprivation came back after I stopped nursing and tried to lose some weight. Depression set in during my son's second year something fierce. I'm sure the experience was part biology, part cultural. I worked too much; we struggled financially. I think my husband and I both felt trapped; the old feeling of not being worthy of food played back. And for me, that feeling is chased by a righteous rage that yes, indeed, fuck you—I will live. The internal conflict became unbearable and at twenty-five, before my son was four, I made a serious commitment to love myself as is and never diet again. I made a commitment not to eradicate myself through deprivation. Although I have my moments of feeling virtue in hunger, I've never dieted again.

That's already weird—having a mom who doesn't diet. That's how my son grew up.

He told me that when he was small, he didn't even know I was fat. I weighed between 280 and 315 pounds during that time. To him, being fat meant having a big belly and I didn't have one, so he just didn't notice that I was... different. I was his mom, likely invisible in familiarity. When he commented on this recently, he wondered aloud whether families who tend to be fatter ever speak to their children about the effects of fat stigma in the same way that black families might speak to their children about being safe around the police in a racist culture, for instance. Sure, a fat kid can be an anomaly in a family, but not always. I pondered this and said no. I didn't think those conversations were common, primarily because a dieting mom is the American norm. Fat stigma is so internalized that an entire family of fatties being radicalized in that way would be unlikely. It's a sad thought; I hope it's changing.

My son remembers other people—his father in particular—warning him about his genetic propensity to become fat like his mother. To them, that meant he simply had to work harder and guard against a dangerous possibility. That's how he learned I was a bad sort of different, as a middle schooler, from other people wanting to police his body.

Because I gave up dieting in favour of an "eat-what-I-crave when I'm hungry and until I'm full" philosophy when my son was so young, he never knew a dieting mother. And although my commitment to eating, shame free, in full view of others was shocking to some, my son reported trusting it. "Sure," he said. "People saw you eat cake and cookies, and sometimes said they worried about your health, but what they didn't see was Dad's diet-and-binge ways of relating to ice-cream, for instance. Dad stayed fit looking, so no one ever knew his actual relationship to food. I think I got some of those habits from him. From you, I saw more balance."

Now in his mid-twenties, he notices that most people seem afraid to have sugary or fat-filled foods around—as if they have to eat them all because they can't stand for them to just be there. When he brings a box of donuts into work, everyone acts like they hate him, even though they eat the donuts. This is culturally normal. Junk food is both sinful and desirable. The relationship with food is obsessive. In those real-time moments of obsession, the focus isn't even on getting fat; it's on consumption. The food itself needs to be managed. Eat the donuts. Ignore the donuts. Rearrange the donuts in the box after taking just a half. This disordered relationship with food is related to fear of fat, but it is also separable in real time.

I'm glad he saw me have an easier relationship with food than many other adults have, and I still have those feelings of obsession too. Because I was a fat kid who turned into a fat adult, I don't always feel worthy of eating anything. That's a tough thing to discuss, especially when it's happening. I'm not sure I ever discussed it with him. He didn't know the younger me who could keep from eating for weeks at a time and who would pass out from hunger and thirst rather than succumb to human needs. He didn't know the slightly older younger me who angrily rebelled against a culture that wanted me to disappear because I had a fat body. That character in me screamed, "Watch me eat cake, fuckers! Watch me lick the frosting from my fingers and reach for a second slice if I want to. Oh yeah, you know you want to watch!" In a culture that has conflated sin with both sex and dessert, I was defiant in both landscapes. "You know you want it! Sex! Cake! You want to be me, and you want to be this cake I'm eating." My consumption became performative and, interestingly, trustworthy to my son. What you see is what you get in this relationship—sometimes excess, sometimes prudence, but an honest relationship, unhinged from social shame as much as I could muster.

Women suffer from both the conflation of food and desire and the conflation of sex and desire. Food and sex are the two ways that women are meant to remain virtuous, nice, pure, and abstinent. These messages are everywhere in our culture. It's strange terrain for a child to navigate with a mother, and it's where I lived, especially when he was little.

I've always known—even in moments when I eat more than my body wants—that choosing to eat is the healthier response to difficult feelings than choosing not to eat. Choosing sexuality is a healthier response to internal pain and external disdain than shutting down sensual desire. When I can't find balance—even still, decades later—eating is better than not eating. I don't encourage that paradoxically virtue-filled, death-wish feeling that comes with deprivation. I want to live.

I forget sometimes that my son has not known me all my life.

Becoming Grandmother in Familial Context

When my grandson was two, he and his parents visited me in Hawaii. We spent much of that visit in our bathing suits, in and out of the water. The baby was still in a diaper with no need for other clothes in a climate where the air caresses the skin. On the first day of that visit, my son's partner innocently posted a family picture of us on Facebook and, of course, she tagged me. I started that Facebook page primarily to communicate with the people who read my essays and attend my performances and lectures. Since then, I've come to enjoy staying in touch with many of the people I meet in my travels. Still, I have thousands of Facebook friends whom I don't even know.

There had never been a picture of me in a bathing suit that was so available to so many people. If I was younger and part of the selfie generation, I could well be a selfie-fatkini activist, but I'm not. I write and speak about weight stigma, about bodies in culture, and about the value of creating new cultural patterns. Why did I ask her to take the picture down? It took a few hours to handle my initial freak out and then I asked her instead to untag me rather than remove such a nice photo entirely. I felt embarrassed by my request. I was shocked that my snap reaction to being seen in a normal, joyful family moment was to hide my body.

That's the power of cultural conditioning. And mostly, I'm gentle with myself. I don't always choose the challenging route. If I'm feeling tired or vulnerable, I don't put my body on display unnecessarily. I don't always have to fight the good fight. But when it comes to my kids, I feel a failure if I don't. I want to be a positive part of what my grandson learns about bodies.

As a parent, my son will pass on messages about the body, about stigma, about size, and about food to his own son, both by example and with his words. If I were parenting my eighth-grade son now, I'd probably be capable of having those talks with him that he fantasizes fat families could have—to prepare their children for social norms and values about fat bodies—to mitigate the harm of fat stigma. He was chubby then, and kids teased him for having man boobs. Shortly, he added a foot in height and became slender once more. He recalls being comforted by another family member's simple comment that his boy-fat phase seemed to be ending. He understood that he was not uniquely failing at having the right body. He was maturing normally through a phase.

I didn't talk about his body because he looked fine to me. I was the fat one. I wanted to shield him from comments like the ones his grandmother made about me. I didn't want him to fear my death. I didn't yet know that some family members assumed him to be also defective because of my presumed bad genes and bad habits.

I hope I've passed along more than my genetic propensities regarding fat. At different times in my life, I've had different language with which to discuss fat. It was enough, in my early twenties, to give up dieting and become stalwart about my own worth and survival. A lot can be conveyed to children without words. And what my son passes on to his son will be complex. His lessons may also include the kind of stories I couldn't tell. He may actually say words that explore personal pain and social stigma, and how they interact with health and kindness and worth.

My son may ask his own child questions I didn't think to ask him, like "How do you feel about your own body, and how others view it?" As he grew, we spoke openly about racism and social class, gender identity, and ability. I stopped short of talking about fat stigma with him, even though I wrote about it for adult audiences. I hope that he'll do better at connecting the tough questions about his own body with the tough questions about other people's bodies. He already has a more complex schema for talking and listening and making meaning to offer his own son than I had to offer him.

He will do his flawed best, along with his partner, who has her own familial context with which to grapple regarding fat and body stigma. I will continue to do my flawed best as well. I'm still better at handling tough topics in writing, in planned interactions, than in off-the-cuff moments when my body feels revealed.

Parenting possibilities continue to unfold; I'm not dead yet. I will continue to do my part with my grandchildren and perhaps greatgrandchildren. My nasty old body-policing mother-in-law was wrong, I hope, about my early death.

I'm definitely a different grandmother than my son had. Both in body and mind, I'm different. I'll continue offering both the live performance of my body—the performance of dignity in difference—and I'm already relaxing more about photographs too. I'll continue to show evidence of self-love, along with passing on clear messages about self-love when I can. So will my son and his partner. My grandson's body will bear this understanding and, hopefully, less social stigma as a result of our efforts.

Notes on Contributors

Sam Abel is a social worker, a PhD candidate, and an artist. Her social work practice focuses on body acceptance, mental health, and refugee settlement. Sam's academic research explores the experiences of fat people in healthcare and in the fashion industry. You can see more of her artistic work @saucy.nudles.

R.A. is an emerging multidisciplinary artist based in Toronto. Her practice covers themes such as identity, politics, history, mental health, dreams, and the body.

bathbunny: Rosie is a freelance artist focusing on cute and fun artwork, spanning from colourful paintings to pencil crayons, and some digital work. She likes to play video games and watch cartoons in her spare time, which inspire her work. You can see her work on Instagram @bathbunny.

Jodi Christie is a solo parent to four-year-old Atticus and works in Broadcast Media to support her expensive travelling habit. She is a feminist, an all-season cyclist, and a sandwich aficionado. In her spare time, she answers the question "but why?" approximately three hundred times per day.

Kimberly Dark is a writer, professor, storyteller, and parent. She helps audiences discuss bodies in culture using humour and intimacy. Her storytelling performances have been invited to hundreds of venues around the world during the past two decades, and her work appears in a variety of print and online publications. She teaches in sociology and women's studies at Cal State San Marcos. Learn more at www.kimberlydark.com.

Megan Davidson, PhD, is a Brooklyn-based labour/postpartum doula who has attended about 450 births and has assisted over 1000 families postpartum. Her research interests include sexed bodies and gender identities, reproduction and procreation, fatphobia and body positivity, the expertise of doulas, and activism and social change.

Emma Day is an Anishinaabe artist and illustrator from Toronto. Her art is shaped by her dedication to social justice and decolonial-intersectional politics, as well as her own experiences as a queer, mixed-blood Ojibwe woman. She focuses on creating work full of hope, joy, and good medicine.

Natasha Galarraga is thirty-five years old and over two hundred pounds and growing. She has been "overweight" her entire life and at the age of twenty was diagnosed with a condition called polycystic ovarian syndrome (PCOS). She lives and works in Mississauga, Ontario. This is her first time contributing a written work to a publisher and her first time writing openly about being fat and living with PCOS.

April M. Herndon currently teaches in the English Department at Winona State University. Her work on fatness has been published in numerous journals and anthologies. Her monograph, *Fat Blame: How the War on "Obesity" Harms Women and Children* came out in 2014 from University Press of Kansas.

Crystal Kotow is a PhD candidate at York University researching in the areas of fat studies, embodiment theory, affect theory, and antiracist feminism. Her doctoral work examines fat-specific spaces as affective environments, exploring the relationship between affect and fat embodiment.

Jennifer Lee, PhD, is a lecturer in creative writing, literary studies, and gender studies at Victoria University in Melbourne, Australia. Her research field is the interdisciplinary crossover between fat Studies and creative writing. She is a queer, fat mother and a fat activist. Her most recent publications include 'Hidden and Forbidden: Alter Egos, Invisibility Cloaks and Psychic Fat Suits' in *Fat Sex: New Directions in Theory and Activism* (2015), and "All the Way from B(lame) to A(cceptance): Diabetes, Health and Fat Activism" in *The Politics of Size: Perspectives from the Fat Acceptance Movement* (2015).

Sarah Lewin, LMSW, is a New York based labour doula and Anthropology graduate student at The New School for Social Research. Sarah is interested in the intersection of personal and public dialogues around health, weight, and identity.

Emily R.M. Lind is a doctoral candidate at Carleton University's Institute for Comparative Studies in Literature, Art, and Culture. Her research examines the intersections between identity, materiality, power, and knowledge production in interdisciplinary contexts. She is currently writing her dissertation on settler colonialism and the Canadian arts and crafts movement.

Liz Nelson Liz Nelson is a recovering academic who now works as a science advisor for Parks Canada. She has never published outside of the biological sciences, so this is definitely a first! She lives in Vancouver with her wife and daughter.

George Parker is a sociologist, registered midwife, and women's health activist living in Auckland, New Zealand. George is completing a PhD in the School of Social Sciences at the University of Auckland and their research interests include the politics of women's health; gender, queer, and intersectional perspectives on health and embodiment; critiques of medicalization; critical public health; and reproductive justice. George is also the parent of two lovely humans, Bell and Mae.

Cat Pausé is the lead editor of *Queering Fat Embodiment* (2014). A senior lecturer in human development and fat studies researcher at Massey University in New Zealand, her research focuses on the effects of spoiled identities on the health and wellbeing of fat individuals. Her work appears in scholarly journals such as *Feminist Review* and *Narrative Inquiries in Bioethics,* as well as online in *The Huffington Post* and *The Conversation*, among others.

Jen Rinaldi is an assistant professor in the legal studies program at the University of Ontario Institute of Technology. She earned a doctoral degree in critical disability studies at York University in 2013, and a master's degree in philosophy at the University of Guelph in 2007. Funded by the Women's College Hospital, her current work engages with narrative and arts-based methodologies to deconstruct eating disorder recovery, and to reimagine recovery in relation to the queer community. Rinaldi also works in collaboration with Recounting Huronia—a SSHRC-funded, arts-based collective that explores and stories traumatic histories of institutionalization.

Sid Robitaille (Sitka) is a burgeoning artist in Southern Ontario. Her work most often focuses on portraits, and frequently walks the line between ethereal beauty and dark and brooding badassery. She is a mother to one small, yappy dog.

deborah schnitzer's novel *jane dying again* emerged in the Spring of 2016 and a feature film *Before Anything You Say* was released in the fall of 2016. Her work includes award winners *The Madwoman in the Academy: 43 Women Boldly take on the Ivory Tower,* and the novel *An Unexpected Break in the Weather.* She is a national 3M teaching fellow and professor emerita who retired from the University of Winnipeg having found in the art and practice of experiential learning in comm-unity irrepressible joy.

Judy Verseghy is a researcher, community builder, and mother. Her work spans a variety of areas including disability, fatness, and mother-hood—all of which reflect various aspects of her lived experience. She holds an MA in critical disability studies from York University, and is constantly toying with the idea of going back for a PhD.

Samantha Walsh is a scholar and activist. She is currently a doctoral candidate at the University of Toronto-OISE in the Department of Humanities, Social Sciences, and Social Justice Education. Her doctoral research is in interpretive sociology with a focus on disability and social inclusion. She holds a master's degree in critical disability studies from York University. Walsh completed her undergraduate degree in soci-ology at the University of Guelph. She is also the co-host of a blog *East meets West: A Canadian Perspective on Disability Issues in Canada and around the World,* found at eastmeetswexx.blogspot.ca/

Sherezada Windham-Kent writes fiction, comics, screenplays, and creative essays, most recently for RaisingMothers.com and Red Stylo Media's comic anthology *The Strip.* She wrote, directed, and produced a short zombie comedy—*Everything I Needed to Know about Zombies I Learned from the Movies*—that played at film festivals across the U.S. and on local TV. She lives in the San Francisco Bay Area with her husband and two sons.